Understanding and Using The British Legal System

Jeremy Farley

Editor: Roger Sproston

Easyway Guides

© Straightforward Co Ltd 2020

ISBN
978-1-913342-46-3

Printed by 4edge www.4edge.co.uk

Cover design by BW Studio Derby

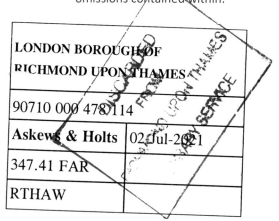

CONTENTS

Introduction

****

INTRODUCTION

We are all bound by the law and the British legal system. The framework of the law affects us in many ways, directly and indirectly. Right throughout our lives we will need to have a basic knowledge of the law. In this way, we can operate as citizens more effectively and we can also have a greater understanding of our rights and obligations.

The book, updated to **2020**, is not a detailed textbook on the law. The purpose is to outline the law, in enough depth, and ensuring that the reader has understood the law and can then apply that law in a practical way.

This book covers, in the main, the legal system as it operates in England and Wales, although there is reference to Scottish and Northern Irish Law throughout.

This edition has been revised in the light of the UK voting to leave the EU and also the advent of **COVID 19** and its effects on the legal system. The main effect has been on access to justice and also the increasing backlog of cases building up, and the need to hear those cases.

The book is divided into 6 parts, dealing with the legal system and how to use it, consumer law, the family, bereavement law, housing law and also access to housing and finally, the police and your rights.

No book can cover all the law, and if it try's then it will be diluted to such an effect as to be worthless. An attempt has been made here to outline the operation of the legal system and also to describe the players in that system, such as solicitors and barristers and to describe the framework of financial aid that can be accessed through the legal help scheme. There is a detailed chapter on putting together a small claim and going to court with that claim.

For many people, the small claims court is the most common method of seeking redress against an individual or company.

The chapters that follow cover accidents and compensation, Divorce and the law, including Civil partnerships and same Sex couples, the law and the consumer, legal relationship between children and adults, financial provisions for children. We are also including a new section on landlord and tenant, given the importance of housing and housing rights in the current day. We also cover the law and neighbours, landlord and tenant and, finally, the law and the police, what to do if you are arrested and how to complain.

The more complicated our society becomes, the more it becomes controlled by laws and regulations, the more that the individual needs to know to be able to be effective. This book cannot hope to be totally comprehensive but does cover as many key areas as possible.

Jeremy Farley 2020

Chapter.1

Understanding the Legal System-How it Works

HM Courts and Tribunals Services is an arm of the Ministry of Justice. The agency is responsible for the administration of criminal, civil and family courts and tribunals in England and Wales. and non-devolved tribunals in Scotland and Northern Ireland. For more information on HM Courts and Tribunal Service, go to www.gov.uk/organisations/hm-courts-and-tribunals-service.

This book deals mainly with the legal systems in England and Wales and there are separate legal processes and systems in Scotland and Northern Ireland.

Before deciding to embark upon legal action, whether you are doing so without the aid of a solicitor, or with a solicitor, it is essential to understand the workings of the British legal system. Only then can you begin to conduct a case or to understand how to get the most out of the system.

Problems arising because of COVID 19
The legal profession, particularly the court system has been badly affected because of the pandemic in 2020. At the time of writing it (the Coronavirus) has caused a massive backlog in hearing court cases and several suggestions have been put forward.

The setting up of Remote courts
The response to an investigation of the possibility of setting up remote High Court has been overwhelmingly positive, according to a report on the effects of the Covid-19 lockdown. Nearly 80 per

cent respondents in the survey, which questioned judges, lawyers and ordinary people who have used the digital civil courts, thought that the system brought in rapidly to stem the spread of coronavirus had worked well. The response prompted one prominent legal technology guru to redouble his calls for a digital revolution, calling for "the widespread industrialisation of remote hearings". The report from The Civil Justice Council, which surveyed 1,000 people, found that those who had used the Chancery division of the High Court were the most enthusiastic – about 84 per cent described their experiences of remote hearings as positive or very positive.

The Queen's Bench division also got strong results; 79 per cent of those surveyed had a positive reaction. There was more unease farther down the hierarchy. Only 66 per cent of feedback about the county courts was positive and 17 per cent of people had negative or very negative experiences. One finding in the report that could provide ammunition to those lobbying against remote hearings is that they do not always save money. Some respondents reported that remote hearings were more expensive because of the increased time they were required to spend on preparation. More advance work was needed, they said, because preparing electronic bundles and documents was more time- consuming. Arranging the logistics of the remote hearings also ate up more time because equipment needed to be tested. Most negative responses were down to difficulties with technology and communication. 'Not being able to see the judge and other participants made it harder to engage and communicate well, making it harder to know how to present a case and when to speak. There were also complaints over difficulties in exchanging documents and taking instructions from clients and most respondents felt audio or video trials worked well for simple cases but not those involving complex or contentious matters.

Nightingale Courts

"Nightingale' courts will tackle backlog of half a million cases

Emergency Nightingale-style courts are to be opened to help to tackle a backlog of more than half a million criminal cases that have built up as a result of the coronavirus pandemic. Ten sites have been identified after officials from the Ministry of Justice searched the country for suitable accommodations, including in the town halls and university lecture theatres where cases could be held within social distancing guidelines. Ministers are expected to announce the first tranche of venues where justice will be dispensed outside the usual court sitting, with more to be identified in the next few weeks. It is hoped that some of the new sites will be able to start hearing cases by August. Although the proposed venues have become known as so-called Nightingale courts, after the name used for the emergency coronavirus hospitals, Robert Buckland, the lord chancellor, would like them to be called Blackstone courts after William Blackstone, the 18th-century jurist. Blackstone was judge, jurist and Tory politician who made commentaries *on the Laws of England* which described the doctrines of English laws. Six QCs say in a letter to *The Times* that Nightingale courts offer a short-term fix but that in the long term the solution to the problems of the justice system is proper funding after a decade of cuts. In their letter they say that they have identified empty buildings which could be opened up for trials so that victims, witnesses and defendants do not have to wait even longer than they did before the coronavirus crisis. More than half a million criminal cases are now in a backlog which has built up after courts had to largely stop work because of emergency measures to tackle the pandemic. The number of cases waiting to be dealt with in magistrates' courts in England and Wales has risen by 22 per cent while the backlog in serious cases handled in the crown courts has risen by 4 per cent. Outstanding cases in the magistrates courts rose to 484,000 between March 8 and May 17, according to provisional figures released by the Ministry of Justice. The number in the crown courts rose to about 41,000. About 250 trials on average a week were removed from a listing before the case was to start between January and March 22, rising to about 400 between March 29 and May31. Trials have started at a number of places including the Old Bailey as restrictions have eased but the Ministry of Justice said the level remains low. Mr Buckland told MPs that he wanted to clear the backlog by Easter next year. He is also considering longer court opening hours, but plans are unlikely to proceed. The justice secretary was keen on temporarily suspending jury trials in cases such as "burglary and low-level violence that can be dealt with by a judge sitting with two magistrates. Such a move would have needed legislation for which there is little time at present and it ran into significant opposition within the legal profession as well as Labour whose shadow attorney-general. Lord Falconer, QC, tweeted "Say No". Amanda Pinto, QC, chairwoman of the Bar Council, said: "This latest increase in the backlog of cases in our crown and magistrates' courts is shameful but not surprising, bearing in mind the lack of investment in the justice system over many years. "When cases stack up this much, the impact on the public is a long wait, more concern and anxiety around the outcome of their cases". A Ministry of Justice spokesman said that courts were "facing an unprecedented challenge" and the ministry was working on further measures to "ensure justice continues to be delivered".

Legal terms explained

There is a detailed glossary of terms at the back of this book which deals with commonly used legal jargon. However, it is useful to highlight the most common terms right at the outset, as they will be used frequently throughout the book:

Claimant – when legal proceedings are brought, the person or persons, or organisation, bringing the case is called the claimant.

Defendant – The individual or organisation being sued, and therefore defending, is called the defendant.

Solicitor – a solicitor is the lawyer you will (or might) see for legal advice relating to your case. This person will have undertaken many years of study and passed all the necessary legal examinations. We will be discussing solicitors in more depth a little later.

Barrister – A Barrister is a lawyer who is a specialist in what is known as advocacy, i.e. speaking in court. A Barrister will have been called to the bar by one of the Inns of Court and passed the barristers professional examinations. A solicitor will instruct a barrister to represent you in court proceedings. However, barristers will not normally be the persons giving individuals legal advice in the first instance. The legal profession is, basically, split into two, barristers and solicitors, both of whom are lawyers.

Writ – A judicial writ is issued to bring legal proceedings. Civil cases are started in the courts by issuing and serving a writ. This document is completed either by an individual bringing the case or by a solicitor on behalf of the individual. It is issued by the court.

Litigant in person – a litigant is someone who is bringing legal proceedings or suing. A litigant-in-person is someone who chooses to represent themselves in court, without a lawyer.

Damages – Civil claims in the courts are for damages, which is money claimed from the defendant to compensate the claimant for loss arising from the action of default of the defendant. An example might be the sale of a good that has caused injury to a person and it is alleged that the good was faulty at the time of purchase.

The structure of the court system
The court system in the United Kingdom deals, in the main, with civil and criminal cases. They are heard in either the county court

(civil cases) and the Magistrates and Crown Courts (criminal cases). *Civil cases* are those that typically involve breaches of contract, personal injury claims, divorce cases, bankruptcy hearings, debt problems, some employment cases, landlord and tenant disputes and other consumer disputes, such as faulty goods. These are the cases that are most often dealt with by the individual acting as litigant in person.

Criminal cases are those such as offences against the person, theft, damage to property, murder and fraud. These cases, if of a non-serious nature, are heard in the magistrate's courts. If of a serious nature, then they will be heard in the Crown Court and tried by jury. Although individuals do represent themselves in the Crown Court it is more usual to use a solicitor in these cases.

Criminal cases

The more serious criminal cases are tried on the basis of a document called the *indictment*. The defendant is indicted on criminal charges specified in the indictment by the prosecutor. In most cases, the prosecution is on behalf of the Crown (State) and is handled by an official agency called the Crown Prosecution Service, which takes the case over from the police who have already investigated most of the evidence. The first stage will be to decide whether there is a case to answer. This process, called committal, will be dealt with by a magistrate on the basis of evidence disclosed in papers provided by the prosecutor.

Magistrates' Court

Virtually all criminal court cases start in a magistrates' court, and more than 90 per cent will be completed there. The more serious offences are passed on to the Crown Court, either for sentencing after the defendant has been found guilty in a magistrates' court, or for full trial with a judge and jury.

Magistrates deal with three kinds of cases:

- Summary offences. These are less serious cases, such as motoring offences and minor assaults, where the defendant is not usually entitled to trial by jury. They are generally disposed of in magistrates' courts.
- Either-way offences. As the name implies, these can be dealt with either by magistrates or before a judge and jury at the Crown Court. Such offences include theft and handling stolen goods. A defendant can insist on their right to trial in the Crown Court. Magistrates can also decide that a case is so serious that it should be dealt with in the Crown Court – which can impose tougher sentences if the defendant is found guilty.
- Indictable-only offences, such as murder, manslaughter, rape and robbery. These must be heard at a Crown Court.

If the case is indictable-only, the magistrates' court will generally decide whether to grant bail, consider other legal issues such as reporting restrictions, and then pass the case on to the Crown Court.

If the case is to be dealt within a magistrates' court, the defendant(s) are asked to enter a plea. If they plead guilty or are later found to be guilty, the magistrates can impose a sentence, generally of up to six months' imprisonment for a single offence (12 months in total), or a fine, generally of up to £5,000. If found not guilty ('acquitted'), defendants are judged innocent in the eyes of the law and will be free to go – provided there are no other cases against them outstanding. Cases are either heard by two or three magistrates or by one district judge.

Who are magistrates?

Justices of the Peace, as they are also known, are local people who volunteer their services. They do not require formal legal qualifications, but will have undertaken a training programme, including court and prison visits, to develop the necessary skills. They are given legal and procedural advice by qualified clerks.

District judges are legally qualified, paid, full-time professionals and are usually based in the larger cities. They normally hear the more complex or sensitive cases.

There are approximately 23,000 magistrates, 140 district judges and 170 deputy district judges operating in the roughly 330 magistrates' courts throughout England and Wales.

Justices' Clerks

Because magistrates do not need to have legal qualifications, they are advised in court on matters of law, practice and procedure. This advice is provided by Justices' Clerks and Assistant Justices' Clerks.

Magistrates in the criminal court

Over 95 per cent of all criminal cases are dealt with in the magistrates' court. Magistrates hear less serious criminal cases including motoring offences, commit to higher courts serious cases such as rape and murder, consider bail applications, deal with fine enforcement and grant search warrant and right of entry applications. They may also consider cases where people have not paid their council tax, their vehicle excise licence or TV licences.

All magistrates sit in adult criminal courts as panels of three, mixed in gender, age, ethnicity etc whenever possible to bring a broad experience of life to the bench. All three have equal decision-making powers but only one, the chairman will speak in court and preside over the proceedings. The two magistrates sitting either side are referred to as wingers.

Most of the cases are brought to court by the Crown Prosecution Service (CPS) but there are other prosecution agencies such as RSPCA, Environment Agency, Department of Work and Pensions, English Nature etc.

Where a defendant pleads not guilty a trial will be held where the magistrates listen to, and sometimes see, evidence presented by both the prosecution and defence, decide on agreed facts and facts in dispute and consider whether the case has been proved beyond reasonable doubt.

Having found someone guilty or when someone has pleaded, the magistrates proceed to sentence using a structured decision making process and sentencing guidelines which set out the expected penalty for typical offences. They will also take note of case law and any practice directions from the higher courts and are advised in court by a legally qualified adviser.

For a single criminal offence committed by an adult, a magistrate's sentencing powers include the imposition of fines, Community Payback orders, probation orders or a period of not more than six months in custody (a total of 12 months for multiple offences). Magistrates may also sit in the Crown Court with a judge to hear appeals from magistrates' courts against conviction or sentence and proceedings on committal to the Crown Court for sentence.

Magistrates in the Youth Courts

Magistrates are specially trained to sit in youth courts, where procedures are slightly more informal than in adult criminal courts – for example, magistrates will deliberately talk directly to young defendants, rather than always through their legal representative.

In criminal cases the youth court can deal with all offences committed by a juvenile (someone under 18 years old) except homicide, which has to be dealt with in a higher court. Sentences are quite different in that they specifically address the needs of young offenders. Young defendants should always be accompanied by a responsible adult when they appear in court unless they are mature enough to be considered independent of their parents.

Magistrates – Civil

Although most magistrates deal with criminal work, they also decide many civil matters, particularly in relation to family work. Magistrates' civil roles include dealing with cases such as non-payment of council tax.

Magistrates in Family Proceedings Courts

Magistrates undergo extensive training before they sit in Family Proceedings Courts where procedures are very different from the criminal courts; the court setting is much more informal and ideally takes place with parties seated around a large table. Cases – which can be both public and private – can be very emotional and upsetting for both parties. There is usually a fair amount of reading as both parties file statements and reports. Magistrates always provide written reasons and can be assisted with extra information provided by a children's guardian, usually a specialised social worker.

Who sits in a Magistrates' court

District judges (Magistrates' courts)

District judges (magistrates' courts) are full-time members of the judiciary who hear cases in magistrates' courts. They usually deal with the longer and more complex matters coming before the magistrates' courts.

The Crown Court

The Crown Court – unlike the magistrates' courts, it is a single entity – sits in 77 court centres across England and Wales. It deals with serious criminal cases which include:

- Cases sent for trial by magistrates' courts because the offences are 'indictable only' (i.e. those which can only be heard by the Crown Court)
- 'Either way' offences (which can be heard in a magistrates' court, but can also be sent to the Crown Court if the defendant chooses a jury trial)
- Defendants convicted in magistrates' courts, but sent to the Crown Court for sentencing due to the seriousness of the offence
- Appeals against decisions of magistrates' courts.

There are three different types of Crown Court centre, based on the type of work they deal with. These are:

- First-tier centres – visited by High Court Judges for Crown Court criminal and High Court Civil work
- Second-tier centres – visited by High Court Judges for Crown Court criminal work only
- Third-tier centres – not normally visited by High Court Judges and handle Crown Court criminal work only.
- Circuit judges and recorders deal with Crown Court criminal work in all three types of centre.

Those defendants in criminal cases who are dissatisfied with verdicts may be able to appeal, as follows:
- from the Magistrates courts there is an appeal to the Crown Court on matters of fact or law.
- From the Crown Court, it might be possible to appeal to the Criminal Division of the court of Appeal on matters of fact or law.

- Certain legal disputes arising in the Magistrates court or the Crown Court can be taken before the divisional court of the High Court.
- Matters of important legal dispute arising in the Crown Court can be taken to the Supreme Court (which replaced the House of Lords from October 2009).

Civil cases

The majority of people who buy this book will be taking civil action of one form or another. Increasingly, people are becoming litigants-in-person as this enables people to access the courts and obtain justice without incurring high costs. The only real costs are the court fees (which have increased substantially in 2014) and other incidental costs such as taking time off work and so on.

The County Court

The County Court deals with civil (non-criminal) matters. Unlike criminal cases – in which the state prosecutes an individual – civil court cases arise where an individual or a business believes their rights have been infringed. Types of civil case dealt with in the County Court include:

- Businesses trying to recover money they are owed;
- Individuals seeking compensation for injuries;
- Landowners seeking orders that will prevent trespass.

Civil matters, for example, pub licensing, can also be dealt with by magistrates. More complex cases or those involving large amounts of money will appear at the High Court; the vast majority of civil cases take place in the County Courts. All County Court centres can deal with contract and tort (civil wrong) cases and recovery of land actions. Some hearing centres can also deal with bankruptcy and insolvency matters, as well as cases relating to wills and trusts (equity and contested probate actions) where the value of the trust, fund or estate does not exceed £30,000, matters under the Equality Act 2010, and actions which all parties agree to have heard in a county court (e.g. defamation cases). Most County Court centres are assigned at least one circuit judge and one district judge, but judicial numbers will vary. Circuit judges generally hear cases worth over £15,000 or involving greater importance or complexity. They also hear many of the cases worth over £5,000 but not over £15,000. As well as hearing cases, district judges generally keep an overview of a case to make sure it is running smoothly. They also deal with repossessions and assess damages in uncontested cases.

Although County Court judgments usually call for the repayment or return of money or property, anyone who does not comply with the judgment can be arrested and prosecuted. The court has a range of procedures to deal with enforcement of judgments.

Who sits in a County Court-Circuit judges

Circuit judges are appointed to one of seven regions of England and Wales, and sit in the Crown Court and County Court within their particular region.

Fee paid judges

Various fee-paid (non-salaried judges) sit occasionally in the County Court – Deputy District Judges, Deputy Circuit Judges and Recorders.

District judges

District judges are full-time judges who deal with the majority of cases in the County Courts. They are deployed on appointment to a particular circuit and may sit at any of the County Courts or District Registries of the High Court on that circuit.

A judge hearing a civil case

Before trying a civil case the judge reads the relevant case papers and becomes familiar with their details.

The vast majority of civil cases tried in court do not have a jury (libel and slander trials are the main exceptions) and the judge hears them on his own, deciding them by finding facts, applying the relevant law to them – and there may be considerable argument about what that law actually is – and then giving a reasoned judgment.

Judges also play an active role in managing civil cases once they have started, helping to ensure they proceed as quickly and efficiently as possible. This includes:

- encouraging the parties to co-operate with each other in the conduct of the case;
- helping the parties to settle the case;
- encouraging the parties to use an alternative dispute resolution procedure if appropriate and;
- controlling the progress of the case.

Occasionally, the parties will have agreed the relevant facts and it will not be necessary for the judge to hear any live evidence. The issues may concern the law to be applied or the terms of the judgment to be given. But more often than not, written and live evidence will be given by the parties and their witnesses and the live witnesses may be cross-examined. The judge ensures that all parties involved are given the opportunity to have their case presented and considered as fully and fairly as possible. During the case the judge will ask questions on any point he or she feels needs
20

clarification. The judge also decides on all matters of procedure which may arise during a hearing.

Judgment

Once the judge has heard the evidence from all parties involved and any submissions (representations) they wish to put forward, he or she delivers his or her judgment. This may be immediately, or if the case is complicated, at a later date.

Civil judges do have the power to punish parties if, for example, they are in contempt of court but, generally, civil cases do not involve the imposition of any punishment. If the judge decides that the claimant is entitled to damages, he or she will have to go on to decide the amount. Or the claimant may have asked for an injunction – for example, to forbid the defendant from making excessive noise by playing the drums in the flat upstairs in the early hours of the morning, or a declaration – an order specifying the precise boundary between two properties about which the parties had never been able to agree.

The task of the judge to is to decide on what is the appropriate remedy, if any, and on the precise terms of it.

Costs

When the judgment in the case has been delivered, the judge must deal with the cost of the case. This may include the fees of any lawyers, court fees paid out by the parties, fees of expert witnesses, allowances that may be allowed to litigants who have acted in person (without lawyers), earnings lost and travelling and other expenses incurred by the parties and their witnesses.

The general rule is that the unsuccessful party will have to pay the successful party's costs but the judge has a wide discretion to depart from this rule. The judge's decision on this part of the case will be very important to the parties. He or she may decide, for example, that the unsuccessful party should pay only a proportion of the successful party's costs or that each party should bear their own costs. The judge may hear representations about this at the end of the case.

Small claims in the county court

A case in the county court, if it is defended, is dealt with in one of three ways. These ways are called 'tracks' The court will, when considering a case, decide which procedure to apply and allocate the case to one of the following tracks:

- The small claims track
- The fast track
- The multi-track

The small claims track is the most commonly used and is the track for claims of £10,000 or less. Overall, the procedure in the small claims track is simpler than the other tracks and costs are not usually paid by the losing party. Small claims are covered in more depth in Chapter 4.

The High Court

The High Court will hear appeals in criminal cases and will also deal with certain civil cases. The High Court also has the legal power to review the actions or activities of individuals and organisations to make sure that they are both operating within the law and also are acting justly. The High Court consists of three divisions, as follows:

The Family Division

The Family Division of the High Court will deal with more complex defended divorce cases, wardship, adoption, domestic violence and other cases. It will also deal with appeals from the magistrates and county courts in matrimonial cases.

The Queens Bench Division

The Queens Bench Division of the High Court will deal with larger claims for compensation, and also more complex cases for compensation. A limited number of appeals from county and magistrates courts are also dealt with. The Queens Bench Division can also review the actions of individuals or organisations and hear libel and slander cases.

The Chancery Division

The Chancery Division deals with trusts, contested wills, winding up companies, bankruptcy, mortgages, charities, and contested revenue such as income tax.

The Court of Appeal

The Court of Appeal deals with civil and criminal appeals. Civil appeals from the high and county courts are heard, as well as from the Employment Appeals Tribunal and the Lands Tribunal. Criminal Appeals include appeals against convictions in the Crown Courts, and points of law referred by the Attorney General following acquittal in the Crown Court or where a sentence imposed is seen as too lenient.

The Supreme Court of the United Kingdom

A new addition to the legal structure of the United Kingdom, the Supreme Court of the United Kingdom was established by the Constitutional Reform Act of 2005. The Court started work on October 1st 2009. It has taken over the judicial functions of the House of Lords, which were exercised by the Lords of Appeal in Ordinary Law (Law Lords), the 12 professional judges appointed as members of the House of Lords to carry out its judicial business. It will also assume some functions of the Judicial Committee of the Privy Council. The court is the Supreme Court (court of last resort, highest appellate court) in all matters under English law, Welsh law (to the extent that the National Assembly for Wales makes laws for Wales that differ from those in England) and Northern Irish law. It will not have authority over criminal cases in Scotland, where the High Court of Justiciary will remain the supreme criminal court. However, it will hear appeals from the civil court of session, just as the House of Lords did before. (See Chapter 2)

The Court of First Instance

The Court of First Instance is based in Luxembourg. A case can be taken to this court if European Community law has not been implemented properly by a national government or there is confusion over its interpretation or it has been ignored. A case which is lost in the Court of First Instance may be taken to appeal to the European Court of Justice.

The European Court of Justice of the European Communities

The European Court of Justice advises on interpretation of European Community law and takes action against infringements. It examines whether the actions of those members of the European Community are valid and clarifies European Community law by making preliminary rulings. It also hears appeals against decisions made by the Court of First Instance.

The European Court of Human Rights

The European Court of Human Rights deals with cases in which a person thinks that their human rights have been contravened and for which there is no legal remedy within the national legal system.

The Legal System In Scotland And Northern Ireland

As explained there are different legal systems in operation in Scotland and Northern Ireland.. Both systems are 'Litigant in person friendly' and the respective websites dealing with the legal system offer help and assistance. The protocol for bringing or defending a case is very similar to the system in England and Wales. However, there are marked differences in bringing or defending a small claim, which are outlined below.

Scotland

The Court of Session is Scotland's highest civil court. It deals with all forms of civil cases, including delict (civil wrongs, referred to as "tort" in other jurisdictions), contract, commercial cases, judicial review, family law and intellectual property. Judges will hear all kinds of cases, but some will have specialisations, and there are particular arrangements for commercial cases. All appeals will go to the Supreme Court of the UK. The Court of Session is divided into the Outer House and the Inner House. The Outer House hears cases at first instance (meaning cases that have not previously been to court), and the Inner House is primarily the appeal court, hearing civil appeals from both the Outer House and Sheriff Courts. Appeals from the Inner House may go to the Supreme Court of the United Kingdom.

In the Outer House, a judge sits alone, but occasionally there may be a civil jury made up of 12 people. The Inner House cases are heard by three judges, although five or more judges may hear more complex and significant cases.

The High Court of Justiciary is Scotland's supreme criminal court. When sitting at first instance as a trial court, it hears the most serious criminal cases, such as murder and rape. A single judge hears cases with a jury of 15 people. At first instance, it sits in cities and larger towns around Scotland, but as an appeal court, it sits mostly in Edinburgh. The High Court hears criminal appeals from first instance cases from the High Court itself, Sheriff Courts and Justice of the Peace Courts.

The majority of cases are dealt with in the country's Sheriff Courts unless they are of sufficient seriousness to go to the Supreme Courts at first instance. Criminal cases are heard by a sheriff and a jury (solemn procedure), but can be heard by a sheriff alone (summary procedure). Civil matters are also heard by a sheriff sitting alone.

The Sheriff Appeal Court was established on 22 September 2015 to hear appeals arising out of summary criminal proceedings from both the sheriff and justice of the peace courts. The Bench generally comprises two or three appeal sheriffs, depending on the type of appeal to be considered. The Court also hears appeals against bail decisions made by a sheriff or a justice of the peace.

These hearings are presided over by a single appeal sheriff. The criminal court sits in the courthouse at Lawnmarket, Edinburgh, while the civil court sits in Parliament House, Edinburgh. Civil appeals are heard by a bench of three appeal sheriffs sitting in Edinburgh, although procedural business, routine appeals and appeals from small claims and summary causes may be dealt with by a single appeal sheriff in the local sheriffdom.

Less serious criminal matters are heard in Justice of the Peace Courts at first instance (equivalent of Magistrates Courts). The JP courts are located in the same cities as the Sheriff Courts, but there are additional JP courts in other locations throughout Scotland. From 2008 to early 2010, Justice of the Peace Courts gradually replaced the former District Courts which were operated by local authorities.

Information on raising actions, and further details on each court's jurisdiction can be found on the Scottish Courts and Tribunals Service website www.scotcourts.gov.uk.

Other Courts in Scotland

The Court of the Lord Lyon - deals with matters of heraldry.

The Scottish Land Court - deals with disputes between landlord and tenant in relation to agricultural tenancies and crofting.

Hierarchy of Courts in Scotland

Civil Court

The Supreme Court of the United Kingdom
Court of Session
Sheriff Court

Criminal Courts

High Court of Justiciary
Sheriff Court
District Court
Justice of the Peace Courts

Tribunals and Special Courts

Tribunals
Children's Hearings
Court of the Lord Lyon
Court Martial
General assembly of the Church of Scotland

The justice system in Northern Ireland

Northern Ireland has its own judicial system which is headed by the Lord Chief Justice of Northern Ireland. The Department of Justice is responsible for the administration of the courts, which it runs through the Northern Ireland Courts and Tribunals Service. The

27

Department also has responsibility for policy and legislation about criminal law, legal aid policy, the police, prisons and probation.

Criminal and civil justice in Northern Ireland

Criminal law is about protecting the community and establishing and maintaining social order. The criminal law presumes that each individual is innocent until proven guilty. The level of proof that is required is that the evidence presented should show the person's guilt 'beyond reasonable doubt'. Civil law is mostly about disputes between individuals or corporate bodies. Cases must be proved on the balance of probabilities (more than a 50 per cent probability that the defendant is liable) rather than the 'beyond reasonable doubt' standard applied in criminal cases. In both criminal and civil cases, the courts make decisions on an adversarial rather than an inquisitorial basis. This means that both sides test the credibility and reliability of the evidence their opponent presents to the court. The judge or jury makes decisions based on the evidence presented.

Courts in Northern Ireland

UK Supreme Court	hears appeals on points of law in cases of major public importance
The Court of Appeal	hears appeals on points of law in criminal and civil cases from all courts
The High Court	hears complex or important civil cases and appeals from

	county court
County Courts	hears a wide range of civil actions including small claims and family cases
The Crown Court	hears all serious criminal cases
Magistrates Courts (including Youth Courts and Family Proceedings)	hears less serious criminal cases, cases involving juveniles and civil and family cases
The Enforcement of Judgments Office	enforces civil judgements

Agencies involved in the justice system

The justice system in Northern Ireland is made up of a number of agencies who are responsible for the administration of justice, maintaining law and order, detecting and stopping crime, dealing with offenders and overseeing the work of prisons.

These are:

Police Service of Northern Ireland-Public Prosecution Service

Northern Ireland Courts and Tribunals Service

Northern Ireland Prison Service

Probation Board for Northern Ireland

Forensic Science Northern Ireland

Criminal Justice Inspection Northern Ireland

Youth Justice Agency

There are also a number of national crime bodies that work across the UK:

National Crime Agency
Serious Fraud Office
UK Visas and Immigration
Border Force

****

Chapter 2

The Legal Profession

In the Legal System covering England and Wales, there are two types of lawyers, Barristers and Solicitors. The Law Society oversees the activities of solicitors as well as the legal profession as a whole. The General Council of the Bar oversees Barristers. For more information on the Scottish and Northern Irish Systems go to www.lawscot.org.uk or www.nidirect.gov.uk.

Solicitors

To become a solicitor it is usual to either have a law degree or have completed an extra year of law if the degree is a non-law degree. This is called the Common Professional Examination.

When the course has been completed successfully the student is still not a solicitor. A training contract must be obtained from a firm of solicitors and two years work must be completed. This training period can also be undertaken in other legal organisations such as the Crown Prosecution Service, or the legal department of a local authority. During the training period he or she will have to undertake their own work and complete a 20 day Professional Skills Course after which time the person will be admitted as a solicitor by the Law Society. Even after qualifying, solicitors have to attend continuing education to keep their skills up to date.

There is a non-graduate route to become a solicitor for mature candidates but the process takes longer to complete.

Solicitors who qualify will either work in private practice in a solicitors firm, or can work for the Crown Prosecution Service or for a local authority or government department. Some will become legal advisors to big companies.

Solicitors will work in sole practices or partnerships and the type of work carried out will be varied depending largely on the specialism of the firm. A small firm will usually cover a whole range of matters from housing, family, conveyancing and business matters. It is usual for a solicitor to specialise in a particular area.

All solicitors can act as advocates in the Magistrates Court. After 1986 solicitors can appear in a High Court to make a statement after a case has been settled.

Complaints against solicitors

A client can sue a solicitor for negligence in and out of court work. One case where this happened was Griffiths v Dawson (1993) where solicitors for the plaintiff failed to make a correct application in divorce proceedings against her husband. As a result of this the plaintiff lost financially and the solicitors were ordered to pay £21,000 compensation.

Solicitors Regulation Society

The Solicitors Regulation Society deals with complaints against solicitors. It is funded by the Law Society.

Barristers

Collectively, barristers are referred to as 'the Bar' and they are controlled by their own professional body-the General Council of the Bar. All barristers must also be a member of one of the four Inns of Court, Lincolns Inn, Inner Temple, Middle Temple and Gray's Inn all of which are situated near the Royal Courts of Justice in London.

Entry to the Bar is usually degree based although a small number of mature entrants can qualify. As with solicitor's graduates with a non-law degree can take a one-year course for the Common Professional Examination in the core subjects in order to qualify as a barrister. All student barristers must pass the Bar Vocational Course which emphasises the practical skills of drafting pleadings for use in court negotiation and advocacy.

All student barristers must join one of the four Inns of Court. Until 1997 it was mandatory to dine there 12 times before being called to the Bar. However, students may now attend in a different way, such as a weekend residential course.

After being called to the Bar a Barrister must complete a practical stage of the training called pupillage. This is on-the-job training where the trainee barrister becomes a pupil to a qualified barrister. This involves shadowing the barrister and can be with the same barrister for 12 months or with two barristers for six months each. There is also a requirement to take part in ongoing continuing education organised by the Bar Council. After the first six months of pupillage barristers can appear on their own in court.

Barristers practicing at the Bar are self-employed but share the administrative expenses of a set of chambers. Most sets of chambers comprise 15-29 barristers. They will employ a clerk as an administrator. The majority of barristers will concentrate on advocacy, although there are some who will specialise.

Originally, it was necessary for anyone who wanted to instruct a barrister to go to a solicitor first. The solicitor would then brief the barrister. After September 2004, it has been possible for anyone to contact barristers direct. However, direct access is still not allowed for criminal work or family work.

Barristers can be employed direct (the employed bar) working for example, for the Crown Prosecution Service and can represent in court.

Queen's Counsel

After a Barrister or solicitor has served at least 16 years with an advocacy qualification, it is then possible to become a Queens

Counsel (QC). About 10% of the Bar are Queens Counsel and it is known as 'taking silk'. QC's usually take on complicated, high profile cases. Until 2004 Queen's Counsel were appointed by the Lord Chancellor. After 2004, selection is by a panel chaired by a non-lawyer. Selection is by interview and applicants can provide references.

Complaints against barristers

Where a barrister receives a brief from a solicitor he or she does not enter into a contract with a client and so cannot sue if fees are not paid. Likewise the client cannot sue for breach of contract. However, they can be sued for negligence. In the case Saif Ali v Sydney Mitchell and Co (1990) it was held that a barrister could be sued for negligence in respect of written advice and opinions. In that particular case a barrister had given wrong advice on who to sue, with the result that the claimant was too late to start proceedings against the right person.

Solicitors and barristers summarised

(See overleaf)

	Solicitors	Barristers
Professional body	Law Society	Bar Council
Basic qualifications	Law degree or non-law degree with one years Common Professional Exam	Law degree or non-law degree with one years Common Professional Exam
Vocational training	Legal practice course	Bar vocational course
Practical training	Training contract	Pupillage
Methods of working	Firm of partners or sole practitioner	Self-employed Practicing in Chambers
Rights of audience	Normally only County Court and Magistrates Court	All courts
Relationship with client	Contractual	Normally through solicitor but Accountants and Surveyors can Brief barristers Directly
Liability	Liable in contract and tort to clients may also be liable to others affected by negligence	No contractual liability but liable for negligence

The Judiciary

Collectively, judges are known as the judiciary. The head of the Judiciary is the Lord Chancellor.

Types of judges-Superior judges

Superior judges are those in the high court and above. These are (from top to bottom):

- The 12 justices of the Supreme Court
- The Lords Justices of Appeal in the Court of Appeal
- Master of the Rolls (Court of Appeal Civil Division)
- Lord Justice of Appeal-Court of Appeal
- High Court Judges (known as puisne judges) who sit in the three divisions of the High Court

Specific posts heading the different divisions of the Court of Appeal and the High Court are:

- The Lord Chief Justice, who is the president of the Criminal Division of the Court of Appeal and the senior judge in the Queens Bench Division of the High Court
- The Master of the Rolls who is president of the Civil Division of the Court of Appeal
- The President of the Family Division of the High Court
- The Vice Chancellor of the Chancery Division of the High Court

Inferior judges

The inferior judges are:

- Circuit judges who sit in both the Crown Court and the County Court
- Recorders who are part-time judges sitting usually in the Crown Court though some may be assigned to the County Court
- District judges who hear small claims and other matters in the County Court

- District judges (Magistrates Court) who sit in Magistrates Courts in the major towns and cities

To become a judge at any level it is necessary to have qualified as a barrister or solicitor. It is not essential to have practiced, as the Courts and Legal Services Act 1990 provided for academic lawyers to be appointed.

Lords Justices of Appeal
Lords Justices of Appeal must have a 10-year High Court Qualification or be an existing High Court Judge.

High Court Judges
To be eligible to be a High Court Judge it is necessary either to have had the right to practice in the High Court for 10 years or more or to have been a Circuit Judge for at least 2 years. New qualifications give solicitors the chance to become High Court Judges. It is also possible for academic lawyers who have not practiced as barristers or solicitors to be appointed.

Circuit judges
To become a circuit judge a candidate can either have had rights of audience for 10 years or more in either the Crown Court or County Court or to have been a recorder. The Courts and Legal Services Act 1990 also allows for promotion after being a district judge, stipendiary magistrate or chairman of an employment tribunal for at least three years.

Recorders
A Recorder is a part-time post. The applicant must have practiced as a barrister or solicitor for at least 10 years.

District judges

District judges need a seven-year general qualification. They are appointed from either barristers or solicitors. District judges in the Magistrates Court need the same qualification.

Law Officers

There is a law office within government that advises on matters of law that affects government. There are two law officers: the Attorney General and the Solicitor General. Both are members of the government of the day and are appointed by the Prime Minister. Both will usually be Members of the House of Commons. The Attorney General appoints the Director of Public Prosecutions, who heads the Crown Prosecution Service.

The Attorney General

The Attorney General is the Government's chief legal advisor. He is not a member of the main cabinet. He will advise government on legislative proposals and on criminal proceedings which have a political or public element. He is also responsible for major litigation which involves the government.

The Attorney General is appointed from those members of Parliament who are barristers and he can represent the government in court proceedings. He is the head of the English Bar but cannot practice privately as a barrister.

The Attorney General's consent is required before a prosecution can commence in certain cases such as corruption, possessing explosive substances and hijacking. He can grant immunity from prosecution and can stop proceedings for an indictable offence. He can also instruct the Director of Public Prosecutions to take over any private prosecution.

The Attorney General has the right to refer any criminal cases to the Court of Appeal (Criminal Division) for a point of law to be considered following an acquittal in the Crown Court and he can appeal against a sentence which is considered too lenient.

The Solicitor General

The Solicitor General acts as a deputy to the Attorney General.

The Director of Public Prosecutions

The DPP's duties are set out in the Prosecution of Offences Act 1985, which created the Crown Prosecution Service. The DPP must be a barrister or solicitor of at least 10 years standing. The appointment is made by the Attorney General to whom the DPP is accountable.

The main function of the DPP is to head the Crown Prosecution Service.

The other functions are set out in the Prosecution of Offences Act 1985, which are:

- To take over the conduct of all criminal proceedings instituted by the police
- To institute and oversee the conduct of criminal proceedings where the importance of difficulty of the proceedings makes this appropriate
- To take over the conduct of binding over proceedings brought by the police
- To give advice to police forces on all matters relating to criminal offences
- To appear for the prosecution in certain appeals

Magistrates-Lay magistrates

Lay magistrates, otherwise known as Justices of the Peace sit to hear cases as a bench of two or three magistrates. Single magistrates can issue search warrants and warrants for arrest.

Lay magistrates do not have to have any qualifications in law. They must, however, be suitable in character and integrity and also have an understanding of the work that they perform. There are formal requirements as to age and residence and a magistrate must live within the area where they will sit: lay magistrates must be aged between 18 and 65 on appointment.

Some people are not eligible to be appointed, including people with a serious criminal record, though minor offences such as driving offences will not disqualify a person. Others who are disqualified are undischarged bankrupts, members of the forces and those whose work is not compatible with sitting as a magistrate, such as police officers. About 1,500 new lay magistrates are appointed each year, by the Lord Chancellor.

Duties of magistrates

Magistrates have a wide workload mainly connected to criminal cases, although they also deal with civil matters. The criminal cases involve early administrative hearings, remand hearings, bail applications and committal proceedings. They also deal with debt related civil matters such as non-payment of utility bills, council tax etc. In addition, they will also hear appeals relating to the refusal of the local authority to grant licences for the sale of alcohol and for betting and gaming establishments.

Specially trained justices will form the Youth Court to hear criminal charges against young offenders aged from 10-17years old. There is also a special panel to hear cases including orders for protection against violence, affiliation cases, adoption orders and proceedings under the Children Act 1989.

Lay magistrates also sit at the Crown Court to hear appeals from the Magistrates Court. In these cases the lay justices form a panel with a qualified judge.

The Magistrate's clerk

Every bench of magistrates is assisted by a clerk. The senior clerk in each court has to be qualified as a barrister or solicitor for at least five years. The clerk's duty is to advise the magistrates on questions of law, practice and procedure. The Crime and Disorder Act 1998 also gives clerks the powers to deal with Early Administrative Hearings.

****

Chapter. 3

Legal Help and Advice

For those needing some form of legal aid, there are a number of options. The first option is usually to visit a solicitor to gain legal help. However, it is a fact that many people are put off going to see a solicitor because of the costs involved. In many cases, unfortunately, this results in people being denied justice.

Solicitor's charges will principally be based on the amount of time spent on the case, as solicitors usually charge by the hour. The longer it takes, the more it will cost you. If the matter is complex, a solicitor will usually look at the case and decide how much they will do and how much a junior will cover, in order to minimise the costs. The notion 'the cheapest is best' is not always correct or advisable when dealing with solicitors, as the quality of advice and degree of organisation will vary according to the solicitors used. Usually, larger practices are better able to offer specialist advice and are also better organised and easier to get access to.

Choosing the right firm

The best way to choose a solicitor is by recommendation, for example one that a friend has used. It will be necessary to ensure that the firm that is recommended has the right experience to represent you adequately. In some areas, all solicitors will generally have specialism, such as property conveyancing. However, for obtaining compensation for personal injury, or an employment law dispute then you will need to ensure that a firm of solicitors has this expertise.

Using a solicitor

Solicitors are, generally, very thorough and meticulous. They have to be, given the professional standards and codes that they have to deal with and also because of the need to obtain all the facts. It is important that, in the first instance, you give the solicitor as much clear information as possible. Further ongoing contact by telephone is charged for. Most solicitors will monitor calls carefully and enter these in a log or journal. Time is money, so therefore you should ensure:

- All information is passed on at the beginning
- Do not contact the solicitor too often. Ask for regular progress reports to be sent to you
- Respond to requests for information from the solicitor straight away
- Require an initial estimate and notification when costs reach the level of the estimate

Aim for a friendly, professional and open working relationship with a solicitor as you are both striving towards the same goal, that is to win your case.

Finally, if you search on line then you can access a wide range of solicitors and gain an indication of their specialist areas. A word of caution: you should always be wary of those solicitors who advertise on television. Many will say 'no win no fee'. Although this sounds attractive, the fees if you do win can be very high indeed. If you do intend to use such a firm make sure that you understand the charges at the outset.

In some cases, you may be dissatisfied with a solicitor and will wish to complain or even sue. If this is the case then contact the Solicitors Regulation Authority www.sra.org.uk or the Legal Ombudsman (address at the back of this book) both of which can be contacted through the Law Society: . www.lawsociety.org.uk

Other sources of legal advice

There is no legal requirement to use a solicitor. People do so when they feel that they need advice in the first instance or feel that their case may be too complex. However, there are law centres operating in each local authority area, often offering free advice and specialising in family and community matters, such as health and housing www.lawcentres.org.uk. Citizens Advice Bureau also offer advice and can be found in each area.

In addition, the CAB has online advice which can be accessed through their web site. This is very useful and has written advice on a wide range of areas www.citizensadvice.org.uk.

Some bodies, such as the Consumer Protection Association, also offer advice, again either by phone or on line, about a range of issues affecting the consumer www.thecpa.co.uk. In addition, if you are a member of a trade union you may be able to get free legal advice from this source, Some banks offer free legal advice and it is worthwhile giving your local branch a ring.

Financial help

The landscape of legal aid funding has changed considerably in recent years. The whole area of legal funding, as with all other areas of public expenditure came under intense scrutiny. The bottom line is that financial help for those needing legal aid has been reduced or in some cases eliminated.

Many people will require financial assistance of one sort or another when either taking or defending a legal action. Lack of knowledge and difficulty in meeting costs are the two main reasons for needing assistance.

The Legal Aid Agency

The Legal Aid Agency provides both civil and criminal legal aid and advice in England and Wales:

www.gov.uk/government/organisations/legal-aid-agency

The Legal Aid Agency is an executive agency of the Ministry of Justice. It came into existence on 1 April 2013 following the abolition of the Legal Services Commission as a result of the Legal Aid, Sentencing and Punishment of Offenders (LASPO) Act 2012. It will be necessary to visit their website for updates on the Coronavirus and the agencies operations.

Legal aid for civil cases (non-criminal)

If you need help with paying for legal advice, you may be able to get legal aid. You will have to meet the financial conditions for getting legal aid. In some cases, legal aid is free. In other cases, you may have to pay towards the cost.

Civil legal aid helps you pay for legal advice, mediation or representation in court with problems such as housing, debt and family.

The different types of civil legal aid

There are different types of legal aid which you can get which are:

- Legal Help – advice on your rights and options and help with negotiating
- Help at Court – someone speaks on your behalf at court, but does not formally represent you
- Family Mediation – helps you to come to an agreement in a family dispute after your relationship has broken down without going to court. It can help to resolve problems involving children, money and the family home
- Family Help – help or representation in family disputes like drawing up a legal agreement
- Legal Representation – representation at court by a solicitor or barrister
- Controlled Legal Representation – representation at mental health tribunal proceedings or before the First-tier Tribunal in asylum or immigration cases.

Who can provide legal aid services

Legal aid services can be provided only by organisations which have a contract with the Legal Aid Agency (LAA). These include solicitors in private practice, law centres and some Citizens Advice Bureaux.

How to apply for civil legal aid

If you're not sure whether you can get legal aid, you can use the 'Can you get legal aid?' tool on the GOV.UK website. Go to www.gov.uk. The Civil Legal Advice helpline on 0345 345 4345 can also advise you on whether you are eligible for legal aid (see overleaf).

When you apply for legal aid, your legal aid provider should give you the leaflet 'Paying for your civil legal aid'. This can be found at www.justice.gov.uk.

Civil Legal Advice helpline

If you are eligible for civil legal aid, you may be able to get help from the Civil Legal Advice helpline. The Civil Legal Advice helpline gives free, independent and confidential advice on the following matters:

- debt
- housing
- family
- welfare benefits
- discrimination
- education.

Legal services for deaf people

RAD Legal Services is a legal service providing specialist, independent legal advice in British Sign Language for deaf people. You must have access to a webcam and broadband service and you must be eligible for legal aid. They provide legal advice and representation on the following subjects:

- debt
- housing
- family
- welfare benefits
- discrimination
- education.

You can get further information and help from their website at www.royaldeaf.org.uk.

Legal aid for criminal cases

Legal aid in criminal cases is organised by the Legal Aid Agency. There are different types of help you might be able to get, depending on your circumstances.

You should get advice from a solicitor who will assess whether you are eligible for legal aid.

Free legal advice at the police station

If you are at the police station, you have the right to free independent legal advice from a duty solicitor. This does not depend on your financial circumstances. Your request will be passed to the Defence Solicitor Call Centre. Alternatively you can choose your own solicitor and won't have to pay for advice if they have a contract with the Legal Aid Agency. The Call Centre will contact your solicitor for you.

If you're under arrest, you have the right to consult a solicitor at any time unless it is a serious case when this right can be postponed. You must be given an information sheet explaining how to get legal help.

Help before you're charged with a criminal offence

You could get help with a criminal case even if you haven't been charged with a criminal offence. For example, a solicitor could give general advice, write letters or get a barrister's opinion. This type of help is called Advice and Assistance.

You will get Advice and Assistance if you get Income Support, income-related Employment and Support Allowance, income-based Jobseeker's Allowance, the guarantee credit part of Pension Credit or

Universal Credit. If you get Working Tax Credit, you might get Advice and Assistance depending on your income and personal circumstances.

If you are not getting one of these benefits or Working Tax Credit, you will only get Advice and Assistance if your income and savings are below a certain amount.

You should get advice from a solicitor who will assess whether you are eligible for advice and assistance.

Help with representation at court
There are three ways you could be helped if you need to be represented in court for a criminal offence.

A Representation Order
A Representation Order covers representation by a solicitor and, if necessary, by a barrister in criminal cases. To qualify for a Representation Order in the magistrates' court, you must meet certain financial conditions. You'll automatically meet these conditions if you're under 18. Also you'll automatically meet the conditions if you're getting Income Support, income-related Employment and Support Allowance, income-based Jobseeker's Allowance, the guarantee credit part of Pension Credit or Universal Credit. Otherwise, the financial conditions depend on your gross income and whether you have a partner and/or dependent children. If your gross annual income, which when adjusted to take into account any partner or children, is over £22,325, you will not be eligible for a Representation Order. However, in some cases it may be possible to apply for a review on the grounds of hardship.

If you do meet the financial conditions, you'll usually get help with representation in a criminal case in the magistrates' court, as long as it's in the interests of justice that you are legally represented. This means, for example, if you are likely to go to prison or lose your job if you are convicted.

In the Crown Court, it will automatically be in the interests of justice that you are legally represented. But you might have to contribute towards the cost of your legal representation from your income or capital.

If you have a disposable income above £283.17 per month, you will have to make five contributions from your income. If you are late paying, you will have to make one extra payment.

If you are found guilty and have capital over £30,000, you may be asked to pay a contribution from your capital.

However, you will not be entitled to legal aid representation if your disposable annual income is £37,500 or more and you will have to pay privately for your costs. If you are found not guilty, your payments will be refunded to you. To apply for a Representation Order, ask for an application form at the court dealing with your case or speak to your solicitor.

Advocacy Assistance

Advocacy Assistance covers the costs of a solicitor preparing your case and initial representation in certain cases such as:

- prisoners facing disciplinary charges
- prisoners with a life sentence who are referred to the Parole Board
- warrants of further detention.

You don't have to meet any financial conditions to qualify for Advocacy Assistance, except if it's a prison hearing.

Free advice and representation at the magistrates' court
If you didn't get legal advice before your case comes up at the magistrates' court, you can get free legal advice and representation by the court duty solicitor. This does not apply to less serious cases such as minor driving offences but it could cover cases of non-payment of council tax.

You do not have to meet any financial conditions to get free advice and representation at the magistrates' court. The court staff will tell you how to find the duty solicitor.

Paying court fees if you are getting legal aid
If you wish to start court action, you will need to pay a court fee. You can find further information about court fees on the HM Courts and Tribunal Service website at www.justice.gov.uk. If you're on a low income, you can get help with paying all or some of the court fee. This is called a fee remission.

If you are receiving Legal Representation or Family Help (Higher) you cannot apply for a fee remission as your solicitor will pay your court or tribunal fee for you. If you receive advice under Family Help (Lower) where a consent order is being applied for, your solicitor will also pay your court or tribunal fees for you. You can apply for a fee remission if you are receiving:

- Legal Help
- Help at Court
- Family Help (Lower) except where a consent order is being applied for.

You can ask the court to tell you how to apply for a fee remission or you can get more information and the form EX 160A which can be used to apply for a fee remission from HM Courts and Tribunals Service.

****

Chapter.4

Small Claims-An Overview Of Procedure

Part 7 of the County Court Rules governs the issue of the claim form. If a defence is not filed, judgement is entered for the claimant because the defendant is in default of the obligation to file a defence. If a defence is filed, the claim is in appropriate circumstances allocated to the small claims track and proceeds under the provisions of Part 27.

We will be looking at Small Claims in Scotland and Northern Ireland at the end of the chapter.

The procedure for small claims is informal. The district judge hears the case in a private room although the hearing is now open to the public if they wish to attend, (in practice this is seldom the case). You can claim fixed costs, your own personal costs, witness expenses up to £50 per day, and in certain cases expert fees for reports up to £200 (only if the judge gives permission to use an expert witness). Solicitors' fees are not awarded to the successful party. However, up to £260 may be claimed for legal advice if the claim includes an injunction. You should check these figures at the time of going to court as they are subject to change. This is to encourage members of the public to conduct their own case. The small claims procedure is designed for lawyer-free self-representation.

In certain cases, expenses for travel and overnight accommodation may be claimed. The Court provides standard forms for completion by the opponents throughout a case with the intention that for simple matters, you could present your own case. The same forms are available from the Lord Chancellor's homepage.

Types of Small Claim

Your claim may be for a fixed amount or for an amount to be assessed. In the latter case, liability for the claim is treated separately from assessment of the amount of the claim. In such a case, you would write on the claim form e.g. "not more than £3,000" when the claim is for between £1,000 and £3,000. If a defence is not filed or if such a claim is admitted, you would obtain judgement with damages to be assessed by the district judge at a "disposal hearing". In most cases, you will know the amount of your claim.

Special Features of Part 7 Procedures

- The claimant is entitled to Judgement in default of the defendant filing the Acknowledgement of service and/or the defence, or
- Judgement on liability with damages to be assessed at a disposal hearing

Special features of the Small Claims Track

- Complicated rules do not apply
- The hearing is informal and not in open court although the public can attend.

Completing and Issuing a Claim Form

From 19 March 2012, there was an important change to administration of money claims. If you want to make a county court money claim you must send the claim form to the "County Court Money Claims Centre" (CCMCC) or if you don't want to use the CCMC, then you will have to use Money Claims On-Line (see below). This change was part of

54

improvements to the administration of civil business. Cases will be issued at the CCMCC and where they become defended and ready to be allocated to a track, they will be transferred to an appropriate county court. Claim Forms can be posted to the CCMC at:

Salford Business Centre
PO Box 527
Salford
M5 0BY

Any enquiries on cases proceeding at the CCMCC should be made to the following:

For email enquiries: ccmcccustomerenquiries@hmcts.gov.uk
For e-filing enquiries: ccmcc-filing@hmcts.gov.uk
For telephone enquiries: 0300 1231372
It is important to complete the claim form as accurately as you can. The Claim Form (NI) is shown at the end of this book in Appendix B. The Claim Form changed when the new CCMC was introduced on 19 March 2012.

Once the claim form has been served on the defendant, permission is needed from the defendant to amend it and if that is not forthcoming then you would have to apply to the court. So ensure you have entered the details correctly and that you have named the defendant correctly. If the defendant is a business then it is important to have the correct legal entity of the organisation. Is the business an incorporated company? If it is, then there should be the word "LTD" or "Limited" after its name. A limited company should have the registered company number on its headed paper and so you can use this number to check the full company name and registered office by visiting Companies House website. It is advisable to state the registered office of a company as the address where the court should send the claim. This should remove any doubts of service. You can of course always send a copy of the claim to the trading address after the court has sent it to the registered office. On the claim form there must be a statement of value. The statement of value should be inserted below the word "Value" on the front page of the claim form. The form of wording should be: "Value: £X plus accrued interest and fixed costs.

In deciding which level of court fee the claim comes within, the court takes into account the interest claimed to the date of the claim.

In a personal injury claim, for example, where you would be claiming general damages for pain and suffering, statement of value would be worded, for example, as " the claimant expects to recover between £5,000 and £15,000".

The particulars of claim must be verified by a statement of truth. The person signing a statement of truth can be guilty of contempt of court if they know that the facts contained within the document are untrue. A solicitor can sign the statement of truth in his own name but states that: "The Claimant believes......". A solicitor should check the contents of the particulars of claim with his client before he signs it on their behalf. If the statement of truth is being signed by an officer of a company, that person must be at a senior level, such as a manager or director.

On the front page of the claim form, there are boxes where you enter the amount of the claim. There is a box for fixed solicitors' costs as allowed by the court rules. These fixed costs can only be claimed if you have a solicitor acting for you.

There is a court fee to issue a court claim. The level of fee depends on the amount claimed. The latest court fees can be obtained from the Court Service website. If a case is defended and progresses to a hearing then there will be further fees to pay. The following shows the further fees payable depending on the track the case is allocated to:

Small Claims Track	Allocation Fee (if over £1,500)	Hearing Fee	
Fast Track	Allocation Fee	Listing Fee	Hearing Fee
Multi Track	Allocation Fee	Listing Fee	Hearing Fee

The policy of the Ministry of Justice is to make county courts self-financing which has caused a steady increase in court fees. If you are an individual and are either on a qualifying state benefit or your disposable income is below a certain level, you may be able to obtain a full or part fee remission, which means that you will not have to pay all or part of the required court fee.

To claim for a "fee remission", you will have to complete the relevant application form and supply up to date documentary evidence regarding your finances. Fee remissions are not available for business. If a claim is issued through the Claim Production Centre, then the court fee is discounted. The Claim Production Centre is designed for those issuing a large number of debt actions.

Freezing Orders

A creditor can prevent a debtor from moving assets out of reach by applying for a freezing order. A freezing order is an injunction which prevents a party from removing assets out of the country or from dealing with the assets. Application for a freezing injunction are usually made to the High Court, but there are exceptions where an order can be granted by a county court such as where it is sought to aid execution after judgment. If you are considering applying for a freezing order, it is strongly recommended that you seek the assistance of a solicitor.

Making a Claim Online

Those with access to the internet can start a claim for money online. To start the claim, you need to visit the Court Service website: www.moneyclaim.gov.uk/web/mcol/welcome

The County Court Money Claims Centre is open to individuals, solicitors and companies. It has the advantage that it operates 24 hours a day, 7 days a week and so you can go online anytime and monitor the progress of your case. Also, a change to the court rules that came into force in April 2009 enables more detailed particulars of claim to be served separately within 14 days of issuing the claim. This removed the disadvantage of the online claim form having limited space for giving particulars of the claim. To use "Money Claims Online", the claim has to be for a fixed amount that is less than £100,000. You have to pay for the court fees by credit or debit card. Users of this system cannot obtain an exemption from court fees.

Response Pack

The court will then serve (i.e. post) the claim form on the defendant with a "RESPONSE Pack" containing four forms, a Form of Acknowledgement, a Form of Admission (N9A), a form for filing a Defence (N9B) and a form for filing a Counterclaim (N9B)

Admitted or Part Admitted Claims: Part 14

The DEFENDANT may either

- Admit/Part admit the claim with an offer to pay immediately. The court will enter judgement.
- Admit/Part admit the claim with an offer to pay in instalments.
- If the claim is part admitted, a defence should be filed to show why part of the claim is not admitted
- If the claim is for an unspecified amount i.e. an amount to be assessed, the defendant can admit the claim and make an offer.

The CLAIMANT may then

- File an application for judgement of the admitted claim
- Accept or reject an offer of instalments on an admitted claim. If you reject the instalments offered, the court clerk will assess the defendant's statement of means and make an order for instalments. If you are dissatisfied with the clerk's decision, you may apply to the district judge for a determination.
- Reject a part admission; in which case the claim proceeds as if defended. And the defendant should file a defence.
- In the case of an admitted claim with the "amount to be assessed", you should apply for judgement to be entered for liability. The court will schedule a "disposal hearing" to determine the amount of the claim or damages payable. If an offer is made in respect of a claim for an unspecified sum, the offer may be either accepted or rejected. If it is rejected, the

court will proceed to a "disposal hearing" for damages to be assessed

Refuted Claims

The defendant may as an alternative to admitting the claim:

- File the acknowledgement requesting 28 days to file the defence; or
- File a defence within 14 days; and/or
- File a counterclaim against the claimant; and/or
- Issue a Part 20 Notice against a non-party or a contribution notice against a co-defendant

Judgement in Default

If the defendant does not file a defence within 14 days of the date of service of the claim (or 28 days from filing the acknowledgement of service), the court will at the request of the claimant order judgement in the claimant's favour without a hearing. This is judgement "in default" of the defendant filing a defence. The claimant should file a request for a default judgement after the time period has lapsed. If the amount of the claim is not specified on the claim form, then as indicated above, you should file the request and the court will order judgement for the claimant with damages to be assessed at a disposal hearing.

Defence

The defence is a statement of case and Part 16 requires that it states (a) which allegations in the particulars of claim are denied (b) which are not admitted or denied i.e. that the claimant must prove, and (c) which allegations are admitted. If an allegation is denied, the defendant must (a) state his reason for denying it and (b) if he intends to put forward a different version of events, state his own version. In the case of a defendant who files a Defence, the court will serve a copy on the claimant and the case will be transferred to the defendant's local or "home" court, which will process the claim along the small claims track. If you expect the defendant to file a defence, you will save time if you issue your claim form in his local County Court.

Counterclaim : Part 20

The defendant may make a counterclaim as follows:

- This will be heard with the claim. A court fee will be payable
- If the counterclaim is above the small claims limit of £10,000 the district judge may allocate the claim to a different track.

The defendant's counterclaim is a claim made by the defendant against the claimant, which may be less than his claim, so his claim is reduced, or it may be greater. A counterclaim is a separate action and an alternative to the defendant issuing his own claim form. Both claims are therefore managed in one action or set of proceedings. The defendant is in the same position as the claimant when making a counterclaim. The rules for the content of the counterclaim are the same as for any claim. The claimant must file a defence to the counterclaim to avoid judgement-in-default on the counterclaim. In this respect, the claimant is for the purposes of the counterclaim in the same position as a defendant and the rules governing the content of the defence apply. Counterclaims are dealt with under Part 20. This Part also deals with claims by one defendant against another and circumstances in which a defendant wishes to issue proceedings against a non-party. If you as the defendant to a claim, or a defendant to a counterclaim, consider either to be applicable you should instruct a Solicitor.

Allocation to a Track: Allocation Questionnaire Form
If the defendant files a defence or counterclaim, the Court will:

- Post a form called an "Allocation Questionnaire" (N205A) TO THE PARTIES. This form records the details of the claim, the case number and date of service. The case number is now the reference point for your case and no steps can be taken without quoting it
- Both parties must complete and file the Allocation Questionnaire. The claimant must pay a fee when filing this form.

Directions Issued by the Court
After the Allocation Questionnaire is received, or in default of filing the Allocation Questionnaire, the court will allocate the claim to the small claims track and issue directions. These are the courts instructions as to how the case should proceed. District judges have wide powers to issue directions but for small claims PD27 provides standards form directions depending on the category of claim. The parties may apply for directions using form N244.

Enforcement Proceedings
If the defendant does not comply with a court order or judgement, you must take enforcement proceedings to enforce the judgement.

Small claims in Scotland-Simple Procedure

What is Simple Procedure?

Simple procedure, which applies from 28th November 2016, is a court process designed to provide a speedy, inexpensive and informal way to resolve disputes where the monetary value does not exceed £5,000. A claim is made in the sheriff court by a claimant. The party against whom the claim is made is known as a respondent. The final decision in a claim is made by a sheriff or a summary sheriff. A person does not need to use a solicitor to use the simple procedure, but they can do if you wish. Where the value of the claim is over £5,000 the ordinary cause procedure should be followed. (see below)

Before making a claim

Before completing the claim form it is important that you have tried to settle the dispute. This could mean writing to the person or company you have the dispute with and trying to agree a settlement.

Another option that may help you settle the dispute, before you decide to complete the claim form, is Alternative Dispute Resolution (ADR). Further information on ADR can be found on the mygov.scot website. ADR is also something that the sheriff or summary sheriff may refer you to after you have sent your claim form to the court as a way of settling the dispute out of court. Other things you might wish to consider before making a claim are:

- Is the person likely to be able to pay?
- If a company, has it ceased trading?
- Are you raising the claim against the correct person/company?
- Can you afford the time to prepare your case for the court hearing if the claim is defended?

- Can you afford to pay the cost of having any decision made in your favour enforced if it is not complied with as the court cannot do this for you?

How do I make a claim?

If you have exhausted all your options and wish to make a claim, you will require to complete a Claim Form (Form 3A). Once you have filled in your form, you should print it and either post or take it to the sheriff court that should deal with your claim. Part 3 of the simple procedure explains how to make a claim and what the court will do with your claim. You will need to decide in which of the 39 sheriff courts in Scotland your claim should be brought. In most cases, the court which will hear the claim will be the one within whose area the person the claim is to be made against (the respondent) lives or has a place of business. For further information contact your local sheriff court. Staff in the Scottish Courts and Tribunals Service cannot give you legal advice, although they can help you to understand court procedures. You may wish to consult with and be represented in court by a solicitor, lay representative or courtroom supporter. Part 2 of the simple procedure explains about representatives and what they may and may not do. You will need to pay a fee to the court when submitting your claim form. The current fees can be accessed in the Sheriff Court Fees section. You may be entitled to fee exemption, for example, if you receive certain state benefits. Further information can be found in the Court Fees section and the fee exemption application form .

How do I respond to a claim?

If a claim is made against you, the first formal notice you will receive is a copy of the completed claim form. Contained in the same envelope will be a response form (Form 4A). This usually comes by recorded delivery post but you may also receive it from a sheriff officer. The claim form contains the details of the claim made against you. If you wish to either:

- dispute the claim,
- admit liability for the claim and ask the court for time to pay; or
- admit liability for the claim and settle it before the last date for a response

you should fill in Form 4A and send it to both the court and the claimant by the last date for a response.

Part 4 of the simple procedure explains how you respond to a claim and what the court will do with your response. Part 5 explains how you may ask for time to pay if the claim is for payment of a sum of money and how the claimant can consent or object to that.

Please note that staff in the Scottish Courts and Tribunals Service cannot give you legal advice, although they can help you to understand court procedures. You may wish to consult with and be represented in court by a solicitor, lay representative or courtroom supporter. Part 2 of the simple procedure explains about representatives and what they may and may not do.

What will happen to my case?

You may not need to attend court if:

- The respondent has not sent a response form
- The respondent has settled the claim before the last date for a response

- The claimant and the respondent have agreed payment terms about the payment of the claim

You may need to attend court if:

- The claimant has not accepted the offer of payment detailed in a response form
- The respondent wishes to defend all or part of the claim
- The sheriff or summary sheriff wishes to discuss certain matters about the claim

Should you need to attend court, you will be informed of the reasons, date and time of any hearing or discussion that the court has fixed.

You may be worried about attending court, particularly if you do not have a solicitor or other representative to speak for you. The following may help you to prepare:

- Part 7 of the simple procedure explains what happens after a response form is received or if no response form is received.
- Part 8 of the simple procedure explains the orders that a sheriff or summary sheriff can give to manage or decide a case.
- Part 21 contains a glossary explaining the meaning of certain legal words and expressions used in simple procedure.

Ordinary Cause-What is the ordinary cause procedure?

The Ordinary Cause procedure can be used in the sheriff court where the value of the claim is over £5000. It is also the procedure used in the sheriff court for a number of other actions for example family actions, including divorce, dissolution of civil partnership, applications for orders relating to children eg. residence and contact. The procedure is quite complex and the Scottish Courts and Tribunals Service would therefore advise applicants to seek legal advice.

Which forms do I need to use?

There is no set application form to be completed when applying using the ordinary cause procedure; instead it is raised using an initial writ. There are styles available within the Ordinary Cause Rules, and can be accessed at:

- Initial Writ Form G1 (including Personal Injury Actions in the all-Scotland sheriff court at Edinburgh)
- Initial Writ Form G1A (Commercial Actions)
- Initial Writ Form PI1 (Personal Injury Actions in the sheriff court (other than the all-Scotland sheriff court at Edinburgh))

How much does it cost?

Court fees are payable for lodging these applications in court, and the current fees can be accessed in the Sheriff Court Fees Section (Please note that separate fees are payable for personal injury cases in the all-Scotland sheriff court at Edinburgh).

You may be entitled to fee exemption, for example if you are entitled to certain state benefits. Further information can be found in the Court Fees section and in the Fee Exemption Application Form.

You should note that these fees do not include any fees you may need to pay if you have instructed a solicitor to help you. The solicitor can give you information on these costs.

Small claims process in Northern Ireland

The small claims process in Northern Ireland allows certain types of claims to be decided informally by the County Court, usually without the need of a solicitor or barrister.

Small claims

In general a small claim is one where the value to be claimed is not more than £3,000 and which does not relate to personal injuries, road traffic accidents, libel or slander, title to land, legacy or annuity or any property of a marriage. If the total sum at issue between the same parties exceeds £3,000, the claimant must either:

- proceed by abandoning any amount due over £3,000 (this will be expressly noted)
- issue a civil bill in the County Court for a full hearing (up to £30,000)
- The Civil Processing Centre, in Laganside Courts, processes all cases initially, but if a case is disputed it is then transferred to the office that is specified within the original application for hearing.

There are two types of small claim:

- liquidated - where the amount of claim is set, for example, loans or goods and services not paid for
- unliquidated - where the amount is estimated, for example, damage to property, faulty goods or workmanship

Once a case has been submitted to the Civil Processing Centre and verified, the respondent (the person against whom the claim is made) is then posted a small claims pack giving all relevant information in relation to the case, including a copy of the completed small claims application form.

The court does not pay the amount that is awarded; it only decides who is liable. A Decree or Order made by the Small Claims Court is a County Court Judgment (CCJ) and may affect a respondent's credit status. It may also affect an applicant's credit status if a successful counterclaim is made.

Enforcement of Judgments Office

Before beginning the small claim process, the Enforcement of Judgments Office can search for a person or firm for a small fee. This will show if there are any enforced judgments already in existence against the respondent within the last six years. You can then use this information to help you to decide whether or not it would be practical for you to proceed with this action.

Even if you succeed with your claim, if the respondent has other judgments lodged with the Enforcement of Judgments Office, you may find that you will not get your money back immediately, if at all.

Fees

The fee for your small claim application will depend on the amount you wish to claim. If your claim is successful, the respondent will be ordered to pay you the amount decided by the Judge, plus the application fee along with any other costs awarded. If you are not successful, the respondent will not be ordered to pay you anything and you will not receive your fee back.

European Small Claims Procedure

A European Small Claims Procedure (ESCP) allows for cross-border cases (for example where at least one of the parties lives or is habitually resident in a Member State other than that of the court where the action is brought) and includes personal injury actions and road traffic related claims.

If you wish to issue a small claim to a respondent (the person against whom the claim is made) who lives outside Northern Ireland but within the UK, you can use the Northern Ireland small claims procedure.

However, you may want to consider using a process where the respondent resides to try to claim your money back. If the respondent lives in the Republic of Ireland you may also use the European Small Claims Procedure.

Small claims online

Much the same as England and Wales, this service allows the public and businesses to make a small claims application outside normal working hours and track the progress of the application online.

****

Chapter. 5

Accidents and Compensation

This chapter deals with accidents to a person and the position following that accident. If you hurt or damage yourself or your property through your own negligence, there will be no one to claim from except yourself. However, if a person is injured as a result of the negligence of someone else, there may be a claim for damages against that person.

The general rule covering claiming damages against another is that you can claim damages if:

- You have been injured against someone else's failure to take precautions against causing possible injury to another or their possessions

- It was a situation where a reasonable person would have been aware of the risk of your being injured and

- He or she would have taken precautions to avoid the risk.

What to do after an accident has occurred

The main point is that if you think that you may be able to lodge a claim for compensation following an accident then you should act very quickly. Often, after an accident, a person may be too shaken or upset to act quickly. A person causing damage to another quite often knows that this is the case and will seize the advantage. The following are the steps that should be followed:

- Make sure that you have the name and address of all witnesses to the accident and that the police are called

- Make sure that, if injuries are involved, these are examined by a doctor or hospital and that you have accurate records

- Make sure that you have detailed, photographic or sketched evidence relating to the actual scene of the accident

- Write out a full description and inform your insurers

When can a person sue?

To prove negligence, a person must show the following:

- It was reasonably foreseeable that harm would result from a failure to take care

- There was a duty of care owed to another and that duty was not discharged

- Damage or injury to persons or property from the failure to take reasonable care

Even if a person can establish all of the above, the person at fault may still be able to provide a defence, explained further on.

Time limits in which a person must claim for negligent acts

The law lays down time limits within which an individual must take legal proceedings in relation to negligence. For most civil claims the basic time limit is six years. However, in cases of personal injuries or death, there is a three year time limit, which runs from the date of the injury or when the individual knew of the injury. One of the important points here is that a person can claim from the date that they knew of the injury. So an injury, say from asbestosis, may have started to form many years ago, and over a period of years. However, the claim only has to be made within three years of knowing about the injury. Children can bring a claim for personal injury in their own right within three years of their 18th birthday, Children under 18 years must sue through their parent or guardian on their behalf.

Civil and criminal proceedings

The main aim of criminal proceedings against another is to allocate blame and punish the wrongdoer. The aim of civil proceedings is to compensate a person for that wrongdoing. However, it is true that criminal courts can also order compensation in cases of negligence.

Alternative sources of compensation

Because the law imposes limitations on the time taken to claim and also because there is cost and expense involved in taking a case to court, many people wisely take out insurance. To take care of ourselves, we take out life policies, personal accident insurance, health policies, household and all risk policies and so on. To take care of other people we take out liability insurance. This means in case of accidents, there is a form of insurance that can compensate. Quite often, the only loss suffered by the person causing negligence is emotional. The consequences of what has happened stay with him or her for a long time, depending on the nature of the accident.

Defences to a claim of negligence

Even f it has been established that another person was legally at fault in causing you harm, he or she may have a successful defence to your claim. This can reduce or eliminate your chances of winning negligence cases. The most common defences are:

- Contributory negligence
- Voluntary assumption of risk
- Unavoidable accident

Only one of the above defences need apply.

Contributory negligence

It can be argued that the victim has contributed to the accident by acting in a way that exacerbated the problem. A classic case is where, if you have an accident with another vehicle and that vehicle was driving with no headlights, the fact that you are driving with dipped headlights means that you have contributed to the subsequent damage by not ensuring that other vehicles can be fully seen.

Voluntary assumption of risk

If you agree to run a risk, and an accident does occur then you may not be able to claim against another. This could happen, for example, where you accept a lift from someone who you know is drunk and there is subsequently a crash. You knew of the risk and therefore you will limit your claim for damages.

However, those who put up notices that try to absolve them against risk will find that they are invalid in law. Such notices may be in a car wash or shop and say something to the effect that accidents are not the liability of the owners. In this case, a risk is not being taken by you.

Unavoidable accidents

When an accident occurs because of something or some situation which could not have been foreseen and against which precautions could not have been taken, this undermines any claim for compensation. An example is where a traffic accident took place because of a sudden illness, which is not contributed to negligence.

The occupier's liability

Whether you can sue someone for an accident occurring in the home really depends on the nature of the accident. Accidents occur in the home for many reasons and it really depends on the cause and effect principle.

The fundamental rule when looking at accidents in the home is that the occupier, or person with legal responsibility for the premises, must exercise a reasonable degree of care to ensure that their premises are reasonably safe for others to use. The occupier may not only be a householder. The occupier is anyone with legal responsibility for any premises, be they swimming baths, libraries or residential property.

Only people who suffer physical injury or damage to property can claim. The occupier can be liable if the injury is caused indirectly by the dangerous state of the premises. The occupier's primary responsibility is to anyone who visits the premises as a guest, to do a job, or for some other lawful purpose, such as to carry out a repair. The liability for harm suffered on property also extends to people that you do not invite, such as authorised walkers. Ramblers, children tempted by some attraction, such as a pond or apple tree, trespassers and undesirables.

The extent of your duty and responsibility will diminish with each category.

Accidents in the street

The classic is where someone falls over on the highway or outside a railway station. You may hurt yourself or damage your belongings. If you do fall because of a loose or uneven paving slab, or fall into a pothole then the highways authority may be to blame.

Defining 'highway'

A highway comprises the road that you will cross (carriageway) and the footpath.

Local highway authorities are:

- County councils
- Metropolitan borough councils outside London
- London Borough councils
- District councils or parish councils for unclassified roads, footpaths and bridleways

Motorways and trunk roads are responsibilities of the Department for Transport. All of these authorities maintain highways at public expense and are responsible to those who use them. If the accident was caused by a mains cover or ongoing maintenance and repair, the appropriate organisation to claim from may be the utility company, such as British Telecom.

When a local authority may be liable

The authority is only responsible for dangers arising from the condition of the highway. Not all accidents in streets are attributable to this. The liability of the highway authority is based on lack of due care. If the authority could not have known of the danger then it will have a defence.

The local authorities responsibility will also extend to lighting, objects in the street that could cause damage, and also failing to provide adequate warnings in any other situation that could lead to harm.

Accidents at work

Liability for the safety of the workforce is regulated by a fairly in depth framework of law. This includes Health and Safety law and also the law governing negligence. Obviously, in a workplace there is a greater risk to the individual, in particular depending on the nature and type of work undertaken.

If you are an employer, it is your legal responsibility to assess what potential harm your employers or others might face in the workplace. There is a requirement to decide on the necessary safety conditions and make sure that they are implemented. There are many heavy penalties facing employers who do not comply with legislation and general tests of reasonableness, from being closed down to being taking to an industrial tribunal.

Employers liability insurance

By law, employers must take out insurance to cover themselves against any claims for compensation from the employee. In addition, a public liability policy is taken out to cover the employer against any claims from other parties as a result of negligence. Insurers will inspect a business where there are known risks, such as a chemical factory and insist on compliance with standards, Failure to do so will nullify the policy.

Health and safety legislation

The Health and Safety at Work Act 1974 imposes a general duty on employers to ensure, so far as is reasonably possible, the health, safety and welfare at work of all employees. There are many regulations within the Act, which cover many specific types of business. So, in addition to the fundamental basic requirements that cover all workplaces, there are heavier regulations depending on the nature of the business.

Contributory negligence

Employees have a duty to co-operate with the employer to take care for their own and others safety. Employees who put their colleagues or members of the public at risk by carelessness or by disobeying safety instructions can also be deemed to be negligent and also liable for damages against another.

Staff at risk from the public

Employers can be held liable if they fail to take all reasonable steps to prevent and guard against the likelihood of risk to their employees. There are certain categories of people who are at risk more than others, such as benefits workers, nurses and so on. Any claim for compensation is usually in tandem with criminal action. Employees who are victims of criminal assault can also claim from the Criminal Injuries Compensation Board.

Medical accidents

In the same way as others who are bound by the general rules of negligence, doctors and dentists have to exercise a reasonable degree of skill so as not to cause foreseeable injury to their patients.

It is important to realise that medical accidents do occur without anyone to blame. A simple routine operation can go wrong because of the reaction of the patient. Compensation cannot be recovered in these cases because no one can say that any particular doctor or hospital is in the wrong.

In all cases, liability is based on lack of due care. In some cases, this is beyond argument. In others, not so clear cut.

Establishing cause and effect

It can be very difficult to establish cause and effect. Doctors are often loath to testify against fellow professionals in negligence suits, patients have to prove that the doctor failed to practice an acceptable standard of professional skill which is not easy for a lay person to establish or judge. In addition, courts tend to be more protective of doctors for fears of opening the floodgates to litigation. A victim of medical negligence, or accident has the additional problem of establishing that it was the doctors or hospitals negligence which resulted in the injury. This is a particular problem where the negligent conduct is said to be a *failure* to treat or to diagnose.

If you think that you may have a claim for medical negligence you will need to take legal advice to be able to further the claim. There are many legal practices who specialise in medical negligence and they will be able to tell you whether you can claim.

Defences to negligence

The doctors negligence may be based on failing to provide information to the patient or in failing to obtain the patients consent to treatment. In the case of a treatment that carries some risk, and information is given, then the doctors negligence is reduced in the case of accident. If no information was given, the patient will be able to sue. If no consent at all has been given to a doctor to adopt a particular procedure the doctor is particularly liable. Doctors have also been held to be liable for:

- Failing to investigate the patients medical history before administering further treatment
- Failing to provide adequate information so that those responsible for subsequent treatment are duly informed

Who is responsible? NHS Treatment

For NHS treatment the health authority or self-governing hospital trust is responsible for any proven lapses in skill or care of its employees. It will not matter whose fault or error caused the accident.

In the case of a fee-paying patient, the doctor must be sued personally. If the injury was caused by negligent nursing care the private hospital is sued. All doctors carry insurance under special schemes.

General non-medical safety in hospitals

Security is a growing problem in hospitals. Numbers of people wander in and out of hospital premises for many reasons. However, there have been some horrific cases of injuries to patients in hospitals from outsiders. Again, the hospital is liable for a patient's safety.

Making a complaint

There is a complaints procedure for any person, patient or not, who wishes to lodge a complaint against a specific hospital or member of staff. This does not however, cover financial compensation. If financial compensation is being sought then legal action must be taken.

To use the complaints procedure a person must be a patient or former patient of the practitioner or institution concerned. It is possible to complain on behalf of existing or former patients but the hospital or practice must agree that the person complaining is a suitable representative.

A complaint must be made as soon as possible after the incident. The time limit for complaints is usually six months form the date of the incident. However, if a hospital or practice is unaware of there being any cause for complaint, the six month time limit begins from when they first became aware. This start date must be within twelve months of the date of the incident.

There is discretion to waive the limit where it would be unreasonable to expect the complaint to have been made in time, for example, because of grief or trauma. It must, however, still be possible to investigate the complaint. There are three stages in the complaints procedure:

- Local resolution
- Independent revue panel
- The Health Service Ombudsman

Local resolution
If a person wishes to make a complaint about any aspect of NHS treatment they have received or been refused, they should first go to the practice, hospital or trust concerned and ask for a copy of their complaints procedure.

Independent review panel

If local resolution fails to solve the matter then the matter should be referred to the trust or, in the case of a family practitioner, the local health authority or primary care trust for an independent review. The matter is then referred to a convenor who has a number of options in deciding how to proceed with a complaint. They can:

- Refer the complaint back to the practice where the complaint began for further action under local resolution

- Arrange for both parties to attend conciliation

- Set up an independent review panel which will investigate the complaint

- Take no further action if it is felt that everything has been done that could be done

- If the person is still unhappy then the matter can be referred to the Health Service Ombudsman. There are three Ombudsman, one each for England, Wales and Scotland. The addresses of the Ombudsman can be obtained from any hospital or medical practice. The Ombudsman has far reaching powers at the highest levels and will investigate the complaint, set time limits and advise you accordingly. The decision of the Ombudsman is final.

****

Chapter. 6

Consumer Protection Generally

Consumers are protected by both civil and criminal law. As we shall see below, the general law of contract gives some protection, especially from misrepresentation. There are special rules for consumer contracts, including:

Contracts for buying goods

Contracts for services

Distance selling

Other areas such as package holidays, insurance, food and finance

The tort of negligence gives limited protection where the consumer has no contractual rights. In addition, there is protection from defective goods under the Consumer Protection Act 1987. The criminal law also affords some protection against such matters as trade descriptions.

The law of contract

All transactions between consumers and suppliers are based on the law of contract. Every exchange of goods is an agreement between buyer and seller.

It therefore follows that underlying each exchange is an area of law which defines the rights and obligations of both buyer and seller. The purchaser and the person who sells goods and services are not free to do exactly as they wish after the sale or, indeed, make up the rules as they go along.

The major area of law which supported and assisted consumers was the Sale of Goods Act 1979, as amended by the Sale and Supply of Goods Act 1994. From October 1st 2015, the Consumer Rights Act has consolidated these Acts, along with the Unfair Terms in Consumer Contracts Regulations 1999.

The Consumer Rights Act 2015-Goods

Under the Consumer Rights Act 2015, all goods supplied under a consumer contract should:

- be of satisfactory quality;
- be fit for purpose;
- match the description, sample or model; and
- be installed correctly (if part of the contract).

Rights of a consumer to return goods Under the CRA 2015

There is an Initial rights to reject the goods – an automatic 30 day period to return the goods if they do not meet the implied terms unless the expected life of the goods is shorter than 30 days. This right entitles the consumer to a 100% refund.

Right to repair or replacement - If the 30-day period has lapsed or during that time, the consumer chooses not to exercise their right to reject goods, they will be entitled in the first instance to claim a repair or replacement. This remedy will be deemed a failure if, after one attempt at repair or replacement, the goods still do not meet the necessary requirements.Right to a price reduction and final right to reject - If repair or replacement is unavailable or unsuccessful to the consumer, then they can claim a price reduction or a final right to reject the goods. The reduction or refund can be up to 100% of the product value.

Significant exclusions

Consumer rights are subject to the following exclusions:

- before contract, where defects are brought to the consumer's attention, or if the consumer examines the goods and any defects should have been obvious;
- where a consumer changes his/her mind about wanting the goods;
- if the product was used for a purpose that is neither obvious nor made known to the trader; or
- where faults have appeared as a result of fair wear and tear (only applicable 6 months after the goods are provided to the consumer).

Services

Like the implied terms that exist currently under Supply of Goods and Services Act, the services must be performed to a certain standard. Under the Consumer Rights Act, all services supplied under a consumer contract should:

- be carried out with reasonable care and skill;
- completed for a reasonable price (where no price is specified, i.e. hourly rates);

- completed within a reasonable time (where no timescale is provided); and

- completed in accordance with any information said or conveyed in writing to the consumer where the consumer relies on it (intended to include quotations, assurances regarding timescales and information provided pre-contract to the customer which induces them to purchase services from the trader). This is in addition to any rights that may arise as a result of a misrepresentation.

Rights of a consumer when services do not comply

Repeat performance of the services - when a provider fails to exercise reasonable care and skill or where requirement arising from information they gave about the service is breached. This Cannot be used where it would be impossible to finish providing service to the required standard.

Reduction of price - A price reduction can also be claimed where the service is not provided within a reasonable time; or the supplier breaches the terms given to consumers, whether orally or in writing regarding the standards of service. Can be up to 100% of agreed price.

Appointment of new supplier. Only in circumstances where getting the original supplier to do the work is impracticable or unreasonable, the consumer may have a claim for remedial work by another supplier.

Significant exclusions

Consumer rights are subject to the following exclusions:

- where unless agreed to the contrary, it does not achieve the consumer's desired outcome (provided trader uses reasonable care and skill);
- where it is the consumer who is responsible for things going wrong (supplier should always make notes of instructions);
- where damage is caused by the consumer.
- where the consumer simply changes their mind ; or
- where faults have appeared as a result of fair wear and tear.

Digital content

The Consumer Rights Act definition of digital content is: "data which [is] produced and supplied in digital form.

Any physical media that hosts digital content (such as a CD or Blu-ray) carrying faulty content is still subject to the Consumer Rights Act relating to goods, but content on that item will be governed by the digital content provisions of the Consumer Rights Act.

Under the Consumer Rights Act, digital content must be:

- of satisfactory quality (taking into account description of the content, the price paid and other circumstances such as labelling and advertising);
- fit for a particular purpose; and
- as described (including system requirements and another other information given to the original digital content). Upgrades can add to this description.

Most computer operating systems or games have minor bugs that are corrected over time with patches or upgrades and this will be tested objectively as what is "reasonable" to be deemed acceptable in the context of satisfactory quality.

Significant exclusions

Consumer rights are subject to the following exclusions:

- the consumer's attention was drawn to an unsatisfactory aspect of the digital content before a contract was made (for example if a game is in beta testing where bugs are typically accepted as part of the game);
- where the consumer examines the digital content before the contract is made and that examination ought to reveal the unsatisfactory aspect; or
- where a trial version is examined by the consumer before the contract is made and a reasonable examination of the trial product ought to make the unsatisfactory aspect apparent (for example, watermarks on files produced by the product).

Remedies under the Consumer Rights Act for defective digital content

Repair or replacement - the consumer does not have a choice of repair or replacement if it is either impossible to do so or disproportionate compared to another available remedy. If content is defective within six months of its supply, it is to be taken as being defective on the day it was supplied.

Price reduction - this is only triggered if the remedy of repair/replacement is not possible or where it has been requested and not provided within a reasonable time. The remedy may be up to the full cost of the digital content.

Other remedies

The following remedies can be claimed either in addition to, or instead of the remedies above:

- a claim for damages;
- forcing the supplier to perform the contract;
- a full refund; or
- not to pay for the product.

It should be noted that a consumer can never recover the same loss twice.

"Free" content

The Consumer Rights Act enables a consumer to be able to rely on the remedies provided for faulty or damaging 'free' digital content. For the consumer to be able to do this the digital content must be supplied under a contract where the consumer has to pay for goods, services or other digital content – computer magazines, for example, typically provide a 'free' CD with various software included with the magazine.

Damage to devices

Where digital content causes damage to a device or to other digital content (such as corrupting files), and that device or content belongs to the customer and the damage is a kind of which would not have occurred if the supplier had exercised reasonable skill, then one of the following remedies will be available to the consumer:

- repair of the damage, which must be done within a reasonable time, without significant inconvenience and without cost to the consumer; or
- payment of compensation, which must be given without undue delay, and in any event within 14 days of the trader agreeing to

pay the compensation. The trader cannot charge the consumer a fee for this.

Unfair terms in contracts

The Consumer Rights Act replaces and adds to the current rules on unfair terms in consumer contracts under Unfair Contracts Terms Act 1977 ("UCTA") and Unfair Terms in Consumer Contracts Regulations 1999 ("UTCCR") in respect of consumer contracts. An unfair term of a consumer contract is not binding on the consumer, and the assessment of whether a term is unfair will continue to be based on whether the term under scrutiny causes a significant imbalance in the parties' rights and obligations under the contract, to the detriment of the consumer.

Whether a term is fair (or unfair) is to be determined by taking into account:

- the nature of the subject matter of the contract (i.e. the circumstances of the contract);
- reference to all the circumstances existing when the term was agreed; and
- to all of the other terms of the contract or of any other contract on which it depends.

The Consumer Rights Act will apply to consumer notices (whether contractual/non-contractual, oral or written) as well as consumer contracts in the typical form.

Restrictions on excluding liability

Although the Consumer Rights Act 2015 is not intended to prevent businesses from limiting liability in their entirety, businesses looking to include in their terms and conditions limitations should note the following:

- it is not possible to exclude or limit the application of the remedies for faulty goods and digital content (such as right to repair or replacement) that are implied into all consumer contracts under the Consumer Rights Act;
- the implied term that the services will be provided with reasonable skill and care cannot be excluded or limited for the reasons above; and
- whilst it is possible to limit liability for supply of services in respect of price and time for performance (provided that such a limit will not prevent the consumer from being able to recover the full contract price), any other limitations in respect of service performance would be subject to a test of fairness.

The Act states that if goods turn out to not fulfill any of these criteria you have the right to demand a refund from the seller unless you have accepted the goods. The act provides that goods have been 'accepted' by the buyer where:

- you tell the seller you have accepted them
- you do something to or with them which prevents you from giving the goods back in their original state, such as alter, consume or damage them
- you keep the goods for 30 days without rejecting them

It is a good idea to report the problem to the seller as soon as you become aware of the fault. If you do wish to reject the goods you must give clear notice of this to the seller. If you allow 30 days to elapse then you no longer have the right to a refund, but you are still entitled to get the item repaired or replaced for free instead.

Faulty goods are also often covered by the manufacturer's guarantee or warranty, but this is in addition to your automatic rights retailer. Your rights may also extend beyond the manufacturer's guarantee once it has expired.

How to obtain refunds for faulty goods

If a fault develops soon after you purchased an item, or if it was faulty straight away, meaning the goods are not of satisfactory quality, then you are entitled to a full refund from the retailer.

The legal term to use here is the 'right to reject' under the Consumer Rights Act 2015 as the item was not of satisfactory quality. You must give the seller clear notice that the item is rejected within 30 days for a refund to be given.

To obtain a refund:

- Contact the retailer. Tell them you want to reject the item and would like a full refund. If the item is genuinely faulty and 30 days have not elapsed since the purchase, you should get a refund. You will probably need to provide proof of purchase but remember this doesn't always have to be a receipt. It can be a credit card or bank statement, a witness, a cheque stub or any other evidence that proves you bought the product from that retailer. If the retailer rejects your claim then check to see if the faulty goods are covered by the manufacturer's guarantee. If they are then tell the manufacturer about the fault and ask for a refund.

- If neither the retailer nor manufacturer offers a refund then write to the retailer again formally rejecting the faulty goods under the Consumer Rights Act 2015. Explain that you will take the matter to the small claims court unless a full refund is offered.

- If the retailer still does not offer a refund then after this then you may want to consider getting the item replaced or repaired instead. If, however, you are adamant that you want a refund, you may be able to take the case to the small claims court.

- If you paid for the faulty goods with a credit card and they cost between £100 and £30,000, the creditor card company will be jointly liable with the seller if the goods are not of satisfactory quality and you are entitled to a refund from either the seller or your credit card provider under Section 75 of the Consumer Credit Act. You can also use this method if the retailer goes out of business after you buy the faulty goods.

How to get faulty goods repaired or replaced

Under the Consumer Rights Act 2015, your consumer rights may allow you to get faulty goods repaired or replaced for free up to six years after purchase (five years in Scotland), although the longer you have had the goods the progressively more difficult it will be to show the defect arose as a result of the state of the goods at time of purchase.

If the fault arises within six months of the purchase, and it's not because of fair wear and tear, accidental damage or misuse, then the retailer must repair or replace the faulty goods. If the retailer objects, he must prove that the item wasn't faulty to begin with or that it wasn't expected to last very long.

If six months have passed and something goes wrong, you might still get a repair or replacement but you will have to prove that the goods were inherently faulty, i.e. show that there is no other cause, such as accidental damage, for the fault. To help you prove this, you may wish to obtain and independent expert's report to back up your claim, although these can be expensive. To get faulty goods repaired or replaced:

- Contact the retailer, tell them about the problem and ask for the goods to be either repaired or be replaced. You can specify which you'd prefer but it is ultimately a question of what is more economical from the perspective of the retailer.

You will probably need to provide proof of purchase but remember this doesn't always have to be a receipt. It can be a credit card or bank statement, a witness, a cheque stub or any other evidence that proves you bought the product from that retailer.

- Alternatively, if the faulty goods are still covered by their guarantee, contact the manufacturer, tell them about the problem and ask for the goods to be repaired or replaced.
- If the retailer or manufacturer do not help, write to the retailer and make a more formal request. Say that you are exercising your rights under the Consumer Rights Act 2015 as the item is not of "satisfactory quality" and you would like to have it repaired or replaced.

In your letter, warn the retailer that if it fails to accept to your demands you will start proceedings in the small claims track of the County Court.

- If your retailer still refuses to cooperate then consult our guide to taking a dispute to the County Court and consider taking that route. Bear in mind that you cannot take a case to court if you purchased the faulty goods more than six years ago.

Second-hand goods and sale items

The Consumer Rights Act 2015 also covers goods bought second hand, as we as goods bought at a discount price in a sale. However the requirement that goods be of satisfactory quality does not apply to a particular defect where:

- that particular defect has been pointed out to you before you agreed to buy the goods, and/or
- you inspect the goods before agreeing to buy them and the particular defect is one that you should really have spotted

The Consumer Protection Act 1987

An additional form of consumer protection is contained in the Consumer Protection Act 1987, which relates to the physical protection of the consumer and his/her property from the effects of faulty or defective products. A product is defective under the 1987 Act if it is not as safe as the average person would be entitled to expect.

Whether you buy or hire goods, they have to be safe. If you are injured by them in any way as a result of their hazardous nature, then the manufacturer and the importer (if it has come from outside the EU) are strictly liable for any damage or loss caused to you or those that used the product.

95

"Strict liability" means that you do not have to prove that they were at fault. What you will have to prove is that the product was defective, and that it was this defect that caused the injury, or in tragic cases, even death. Therefore, if you are injured when your car, whether it is your own, hired or being bought on HP, crashes due to a defect then you could sue the manufacturer for your injury and losses. However the Act only applies to damage caused to goods other than those that are defective, it does not allow you to claim for the cost of the defective goods themselves only the damage or injury caused to other goods or people by the defect.

Non receipt of goods and late delivery-Delivery rights

The retailer is responsible for goods until they are in your physical possession or in the possession of someone appointed by you to accept them. This means that retailers are liable for the service provided by the couriers they employ - the delivery firm is not liable. The retailer is responsible for the goods until they are delivered to you and in your possession.

Late deliveries

There is a default delivery period of 30 days during which the retailer needs to deliver unless a longer period has been agreed.

Guarantees and Warranties

In law, a guarantee is an agreement given by a trader to a consumer, without any extra charge, to repair, replace or refund on goods which do not meet the specifications set out in the guarantee. A warranty is an insurance policy which provides cover for the unexpected failure or breakdown of goods, usually after the manufacturer's or trader's
96

guarantee has run out. Guarantees and warranties are additional to the legal rights you have as a consumer and must not affect those rights in any way.

What is a guarantee?

In law, a guarantee is an agreement given by a trader to a consumer, without any extra charge, to repair, replace or refund goods that do not meet the specifications set out in the guarantee. A guarantee is usually issued by the manufacturer of goods or by a trader that provides goods as part of a service - replacement windows, for instance. Generally, a guarantee provider undertakes to carry out free repairs, for a set period of time, for problems that can be attributed to manufacturing defects.

An insurance backed guarantee provides the consumer with protection if the trader that provided the goods or service under guarantee ceases to trade and can no longer fulfil its obligations under the guarantee. The insurance company underwrites the terms of the guarantee for the remainder of the guarantee period.

A guarantee is additional to the legal rights you have as a consumer and must not affect those rights in any way.

What is a warranty?

A warranty (or extended warranty) is broadly defined in law as a contract for cover for goods, which is entered into by a consumer for (money) monetary consideration. A warranty is a form of insurance policy which provides cover for the unexpected failure or breakdown of goods, usually after the manufacturer's or trader's guarantee has run out. Some warranties are service contracts rather than insurance backed (you should check the status of the warranty before you purchase it) . Warranties can vary - they offer different protection, from the most basic cover to those which provide comprehensive cover. For instance, you may be covered only for the 'market value' of the goods, which means their second hand value after use or you may be covered 'new for old'. Do not assume that a warranty will provide cover for all problems encountered with the goods. They usually have exclusions that set limits on the cover you receive.

A warranty or extended warranty is additional to the legal rights you have as a consumer and must not affect those rights in any way.

What legal protection do I get with warranties and guarantees?
The Sale and Supply of Goods to Consumers Regulations 2002 states that if a guarantee provider offers a guarantee on goods sold or supplied to consumers, the provider takes on a contractual obligation to honour the conditions set out in the guarantee. For example, if the guarantee provider refuses to repair goods as set out under the terms of the guarantee, you can take legal action against the provider of the guarantee for breach of contract. This could be claiming back the cost of repairs if you have had them carried out elsewhere.

The guarantee should be written in English and the terms should be set out in plain intelligible language. The name and address of the guarantee provider, the duration of the guarantee and the location it covers must also be given. You have the right to ask the provider to make the guarantee available to you in writing or any other durable form available.

If you have a problem with an insurance backed extended warranty that was sold to you, and you have been unable to resolve it with the warranty provider, you are entitled to take your complaint to the Financial Ombudsman Service. For problems with non insurance backed extended warranties, contact the Citizens Advice consumer service.

The Supply of Extended Warranties on Domestic Electrical Goods Order 2005 requires traders that supply extended warranties on domestic electrical goods to provide consumers with certain information before the sale of the extended warranty.

Traders supplying this type of extended warranty are required to:

- clearly display the price and duration of the warranty
- make it clear that the warranty is optional
- give you information on your statutory rights
- inform you that the warranty does not have to be purchased at the time the goods are purchased
- provide details of cancellation and termination rights
- inform you that warranties may be available elsewhere
- provide a statement on the financial protection consumers have if the provider of the extended warranty goes out of business
- state whether or not the warranty will cease if a claim is made
- inform you that your household insurance may be relevant to the purchase of the goods
- give a quotation in writing and inform you that the quotation price is valid for at least 30 days if the warranty costs more than £20
- allow you to cancel it within 45 days and get a refund if a claim has not been made and if the warranty that was supplied has an initial duration of more than one year

- allow you to cancel it and receive a pro rata refund after 45 days even if a claim has been made and if the warranty that was supplied has an initial duration of more than one year

If insurance backed guarantees and warranties are marketed and sold at a distance - without face to face contact between the consumer and trader, such as online - the Financial Services (Distance Marketing) Regulations 2004 apply. These regulations cover the distance marketing of consumer financial services and specify the information that must be given to you before and after a contract is concluded. You have the right to cancel a financial services distance contract and the cancellation period for this type of insurance is 14 calendar days which runs from the day after the day the contract is concluded. Guarantees and warranties are in addition to the statutory rights you have under the Consumer Rights Act 2015.

Package Holidays

Thos is one area that has been particularly badly affected by the coronavirus. Now that the dust has settled things seem to be getting clearer. Outlined below are the main rights relating to travel. However, at the end of this section I have included a question and answer section, which provides basic answers to the most common problems.

There are various common law protections in the case of holidays. However, the main area of consumer protection in the case of package holidays are the Package Travel, Package Holidays and Package Tours Regulations 1992 and the ABTA Code of practice.

The Regulations were introduced to comply with EU Directive 90/314 on Package Holidays and Package Tours. The directive was inevitable because of the level of tourism across EU member states.

Most consumer problems related to holidays concern differences between the holiday description on booking and the actual reality. It is possible in these circumstances that there is also an offence under s14 Trade Descriptions Act 1978.

The Package Travel, Package Holidays and Package Tours Regulations 1992-The definition of 'package holidays'.
The Regulations do not alter the existing common-law protections but add significant duties on tour operators. The Regulations apply to all package holidays-but the word `package' is given a very broad definition in Regulation 2 (1): the prearranged combination of at least two of the following components when sold or offered for sale at an inclusive price and when the service covers a period of more than 24 hours or includes overnight accommodation:

a) transport
b) accommodation
c) other tourist services not ancillary to transport or accommodation and accounting for a significant proportion of the package and

i) submission of separate accounts for different components shall not cause the arrangement to be other than a package

ii)the fact that a combination is arranged at the request of the consumer in accordance with his specific instructions (whether modified or not) shall not of itself cause it to be treated as other than prearranged,

Information to be given by the holiday operator before the contract is concluded

The basic common law rules on formation can apply. The brochure is generally seen as an invitation to treat. But the Regulations, in Regulation 9, provide certain safeguards by ensuring that certain information is given to the consumer before the contract is concluded, and that the information is comprehensible to the consumer. The necessary information is detailed in schedule 2:

- the intended destination
- the intended means of travel
- the exact dates and the place of departure
- the locality of accommodation and its classification
- meals that are included in the package
- the minimum number of travellers to allow the holiday to go ahead
- any relevant itineraries, visits or excursions
- the names and full addresses of the organiser, retailer and insurer
- the price and any details with regard to revising the price
- the payment schedule and method of payment
- any other necessary details, such as specific arrangements for diet etc, that have been indicated by the consumer
- the method and period for complaints to be made.

This information must be given to the consumer both before the contract is made and in the contract itself. This will not apply to late bookings. Failure to comply is a breach under regulation 9(3) and the operator is then prevented from relying on terms that are not

102

sufficiently explained in this way - and the consumer may also cancel the holiday.

Statements made in holiday brochures

The common law distinction between terms and `trade puffs' applies where no reasonable person could rely on the statement. But, in any case, by regulation 4, holiday operators will be liable if they supply misleading information in their descriptive matter.

Liability-Terms and performance of the contract

By regulation 15(1) the operator is liable for the improper performance of the contract by other service providers. The only exception is where the improper performance is neither the fault of the operator nor of any other service provider:

- including where it is the fault of the consumer
- or where it is caused by the unforeseeable and unavoidable act of the third party; and
- where forces majeure applies, e.g. hurricanes

The ABTA Code of Practice also requires that it should be a term of all contracts for package holidays that the operator will accept liability for the acts or omissions of their employees, agents, sub-contractors and suppliers which results in death, injury or illness-and that the operators will offer advice, guidance and financial assistance of up to £5000 to consumers on holiday who suffer death, injury or illness.

Alterations to the holiday

Alteration depends on the terms of the contract-a common term allows alteration to the itinerary. If an alteration amounts to non-performance then it is a breach of the contract by the operator and will be classed as a breach of the condition allowing the consumer to repudiate and claim back the cost of the holiday.

The ABTA Code Clause 2.4 requires operators to offer suitable alternatives in the case of cancellation or alteration.

Overbooking of flights

Passengers who are denied travel because of overbooking are entitled to a choice/combination of:

- reimbursement of the cost of the ticket
- re-routing to the destination at the earliest moment
- re-routing at a later date, at the passengers convenience
- compensation

There are special rules applying to overbooked flights from airports in the European Union. The rules also apply to flights from airports outside the EU but flying into an EU airport, on an EU airline.

These rules apply only if you were not allowed to board the flight, not if you volunteered to take a different flight. You must have a valid ticket and have met check in deadlines at the airport. If these conditions are met then you will be entitled to a full refund of your ticket and a free return flight to your first point of departure, if needed, or another flight either as soon as possible or at a later date of your choice. You will also be entitled to:

- compensation. The amount you get will depend on the circumstances, i.e. how late you were as a result of the overbooking

- compensation for two telephone calls, e mails or other forms of communication
- reasonable meals and refreshments if you have to wait for a later flight
- Hotel accommodation if appropriate (stay overnight until next flight)

If the above EU rules don't apply then you should check the terms and conditions with the operator.

Remember, the law applies to this area as it does to all other areas and the operator cannot opt out. If you are not satisfied with what has happened then you should contact ABTA who run an arbitration scheme (address at the back of the book).

You can also contact the Association of Independent Tour Operators on www.abta.com.

Insolvency of the tour operator

The Package Travel, Package Holidays and Package Tours Regulations 1992 apply. Under regulation 16(1) tour operators must at all times be able to satisfy evidence of sufficient funds to be able to return deposits in the event of insolvency. Consumers who pay by credit card are also protected under the Consumer Credit Act 1974.

ABTA bonding arrangements ensure that a consumer is not left stranded when a tour operator goes into insolvency during his/her holidays.

Remedies

Damages are usually awarded on the basis of difference in value between what was contracted for and what was provided. Incidental losses are also possible. Claims are also possible for physical discomfort. Operators are, basically, liable for all losses that arise from the breach.

A summary of your rights to a refund for cancelled holidays.

Cancellations and credit

Never has going on holiday been such a stressful experience. You cannot go on the longed-for-trip- and you cannot get your money back either. Here we answer some of the most prevalent questions. Remember, as time goes by the situation will no doubt clear up. At the moment, the government is about to announce the creation of 'Air Corridors' which will allow holidaymakers to travel to those countries that have opened their borders to tourists. These countries include the main destinations for Brits on holiday such as France, Spain, Greece and Italy.

All information below is relevant at July 2020.

I want a cash refund for my cancelled holiday but I have only been offered a voucher. Is this allowed?

No. Under package travel regulations you are entitled to a full refund within 14 days of a trip being formally cancelled. For flights, a refund is due within a maximum of seven days from the date of cancellation. For thousands of people, though, this is not happening – and travel industry is breaking the law. Many firms are offering a credit note, which can be used in the future, but people are understandably doubtful that travel company or airline will still be around to redeem it.

I have a family holiday booked for July. The travel firm is demanding I pay – but am I being asked to fork out for a holiday that will not take place?

Many people are, like you, being told their trips are still scheduled to proceed. These customers are being advised by travel agents to pay the full balance by the scheduled date, as their terms and conditions state. This is not illegal, but customer groups believe it is unethical because holidays are very likely to be cancelled.

Are all companies behaving in the same way?

Big firms such as Tui and Virgin Holidays are officially showing no flexibility in payment due date, despite the fact that it is increasingly unlikely a trip will happen. However, both say customers who are struggling to pay because of Covid-19 should contact them individually to discuss their circumstances. Others firms, such as the school trips organiser EST, are providing more leeway and pushing back payment dates until people are closer to departure dates. EST said outstanding balances would become due only four weeks before departure rather than 10 weeks.

More firms will probably follow its lead in the coming weeks. If you do not pay the full balance by the payment due date and your holiday is still scheduled to go ahead, you will lose your deposit, according to most firms' terms and conditions. On the other hand, if you do choose to pay the balance for a package holiday by the mandate date, all your money is protected under the ATOL scheme, even if your travel company goes bust. So if the deposit was small, you may decide to cut your losses and not hand over any further money. If the deposit was large, you are probably better off continuing to pay.

Why are airlines and travel agents behaving like this?

Simple economics. The travel industry is on its knees and has called for a government bailout to stop a swathe of bankruptcies. As a result, ABTA, the UK trade association of travel agents, has called on the government to allow refunds to be temporarily replaced with credit notes to keep money within the industry.

Should I take a credit note?

ABTA claims credit notes from holiday firms are protected by the ABTA scheme, which guarantees package holiday customer will get their money back if their company goes bust between booking and taking place. The government has not yet confirmed this.

For flights, Rory Boland, of the consumer group Which?, warns vouchers could leave travellers exposed in the event of an airline collapsing. "There are no advantages to an airline voucher," he said. "It either offers no financial protection if the airline goes bust, or it locks you into rebooking with an airline when it may not have the best fare or times to your destination".

I have been told I need to pay an administration fee to make changes to my booking. Is this allowed?

By law, no one can be charged such a fee to receive a-refund-but you can be charged one for rearranging your holiday or your flight times. As a result, several customers say they are being threatened with a fee if they choose to rearrange trips themselves, which is in many firms' terms and conditions.

Nobody ever gets back to me from my travel company. What now?
Be patient, however maddening this situation may seem. Travel companies are under unprecedented pressure, dealing with millions of refund requests with reduced levels of staff in unusual working conditions. Some airlines are more responsive on Twitter and other passengers have reported better success by calling late at night or mid-morning, when lines are less busy.

Can I get a refund directly **from my credit card firm?**
This is a grey area and many credit card companies – already hit in the pocket by the obligation to provide cash-strapped borrowers with payment holidays –are resisting this fiercely. Under section 75 of the Consumer Credit Act, customers who booked holidays or flights by credit card should be able to claim the money back from their card provider if they can prove the seller was guilty of a breach of contract.

I am thinking of booking a week's skiing trip for December 2020. Should I do so?
The risk remains of a second Covid-19 peak, which may result in another lockdown and put you in exactly the same position as summer holiday makers are in now. It would be a brave person who booked a holiday today.

Consumers and Credit
The most important Act dealing with consumers and credit is the Consumer Credit Act 1974 (amended in 2006) the Financial Services and Markets Act 2000 and various regulations implementing European Union consumer credit law. The 1974 Act also encompasses loans from pawnbrokers and also payday loans. This has been supplemented by

the Consumer Credit (Advertising) Regulations 2011 (see further on in this chapter).

Nowadays, many people use credit to help them with their buying. It helps to spread the load, especially with expensive items such as furniture or cars. But borrowing can be costly and with so many different types of credit available, it is wise to shop around before you sign any credit agreement.

Using a credit card when buying a single item costing over £100 but under £30,000 can provide extra protection if you have a problem with your purchase. Whether you use your credit card to pay the full amount or even part of the deposit (as little as £1 but no more than £25,000), the credit card company is legally bound to help in cases of faulty goods or non-delivery if the retailer goes out of business.

Try to avoid interest charges by paying your credit card bill off in full when it arrives. Be warned, however, that you may not be protected if your payment is made through a third party - see the section below on credit cards.

Breach of contract over £30,000

If the item or service you are buying costs more than £30,000, the protection under Section 75 of the Consumer Credit Act won't apply.

Depending on the circumstances though, you may have protection under Section 75A. The price of the item or service must be more than £30,000 and the amount of credit the seller has arranged for you mustn't be more than £60,260.

If something goes wrong then the credit provider could be in breach of contract as long as:

- •you can't trace the seller
- • you've contacted the seller but they've failed to respond

•the seller has become insolvent

•you've taken reasonable steps to pursue the seller but you haven't obtained satisfaction.

But if something goes wrong and the seller offers you a replacement or compensation which you have accepted, you can't claim under Section 75A.

What the law says

The main law to give you protection when buying on credit is the Consumer Credit Act 1974. By law you're entitled to a copy of your credit agreement so make sure you get one. Never sign a blank form or even leave some sections blank.

Right of withdrawal

You have a right to withdraw from a credit agreement without giving any reason, within 14 days. When the 14 day period begins will depend on when the agreement is made and there must be information in the agreement telling you about your withdrawal rights. On withdrawal you must repay the amount of money received and any interest accrued.

Credit cards

Under section 75 of the Consumer Credit Act 1974, if you use your credit card to buy a single item costing more than £100 but no more than £30,000, you can claim from the credit card company or the trader if something goes wrong. Many websites use an online payment processor such as Paypal, Worldpay or Google Checkout. While the law in this area is not certain, you may not be covered by the protection offered by section 75. Online payment processors do have their own refund systems, so make sure you read their terms and conditions carefully. If you use a credit card to buy airline or other travel tickets from a travel agent you cannot normally claim against the travel agent if the airline delays or cancels the flight as they were contracted to supply the ticket, not the flight. However, if you use a credit card to buy the travel agent's own package of travel arrangements the agent then becomes the supplier of the holiday package and has equal liability with the credit card company.

Credit reference agencies

You don't have a right to credit. Before giving you credit, lenders want to check whether you're an acceptable risk. To help them do this they may check with firms called Credit Reference Agencies (CRAs). These agencies don't keep 'black lists' or give an opinion as to whether or not you should be given credit. They just provide information about your credit record.

You are entitled to see a copy of any information they hold on you and to correct anything in it that you can prove is wrong. You are entitled to see a copy of your file if you make a written request and send £2. Online and telephone requests may cost more. The contact details of the credit reference agencies are shown below and you can also find more information on the website of the Money Advice Service. The CRA commits a criminal offence if it fails to correct files.

Credit unions

To borrow from a credit union you must first become a member and show by saving regularly over a set period that you will be able to afford the repayments.

This is an excellent way of getting credit as the interest rate is usually lower than that used by other lenders.

Hire purchase

You cannot end a hire purchase agreement unless you are up to date with your payments. You will have to pay at least half of the total hire purchase price. You cannot sell the goods until the agreement has been paid off.

Logbook loans

Consumers will regularly see these loans being advertised on the high street or on the internet promising cash fast, but they can often prove to be more problematic than beneficial for borrowers. A logbook loan is a loan secured on your vehicle. You will be asked to hand over the logbook (V5 form - vehicle registration document) and sign a document called a bill of sale. This means that the protection provided by the Consumer Credit Act – that cars cannot be seized without a court order – is removed and the lender can then seize the car if the loan is not paid.

The bill of sale also transfers temporary ownership of your vehicle to the lender, but you are still able to use it while you are making the loan repayments. You only become the legal owner of the vehicle once again when you have settled the agreement in full.

Consumers should consider other types of borrowing before agreeing to a logbook loan, especially if you cannot do without your vehicle. Although these loans provide quick access to money, the APR is likely to be very high, commonly over 200% APR. There may be cheaper ways you can borrow, which do not put you at such a risk of losing your assets. The concept of a logbook loan can be complicated, so if you plan to take one out make sure you ask the lender to explain anything you do not understand. It is vitally important you understand your responsibilities under the agreement to help you minimise the risk of losing your vehicle.

Furthermore, the law only recognises the bill of sale if the lender registers it with the High Court. If it is not registered, the lender must get a court's approval to repossess your vehicle. So if you think you may fall behind with your loan repayments and want to know what will happen to your vehicle, you will need to check if the bill of sale is registered. You will need to give both your and your lender's name and address along with a small fee to the High Court.

Money lenders

They charge high interest rates and you should be very careful with this type of credit. Avoid anyone who simply calls at your home or speaks to you in the pub and offers you a loan: they are committing a criminal offence. Money leaders may ask for some security for the loan. If they do, never give them your child benefit book or other social security book.

Payday loans

Consumers unable to access credit through traditional banking means are increasingly turning to alternative sources, including payday loan companies. Payday, or paycheque loans, are short-term loans that you get in return for your pay cheque or proof of your income. They are basically cash advances on the salary you are expecting and are available online and on the high street.

They can be a way of getting your hands on your wages quicker than you otherwise would, but it is important to be aware of the high interest rates charged and the consequences of falling behind with your repayment. This type of borrowing is not suitable for those looking to repay their loans over a long period, as they are designed to be short-term loans to deal with short-term personal cash flow issues. If loans are rolled over, debts could escalate and consumers could get into difficulties. They should only be considered if consumers are confident that they'll be able to repay the debt in full when it is due. If you are considering using a payday loan company, you should look into all the available alternatives first:

- Speak to your bank manager as you may be able to get an agreed overdraft
- Look into Social Fund Loans - these are government-funded, interest-free loans available to those on low incomes
- Check out your local credit union.

If you have no alternative to a payday loan make sure:

- You fully understand the costs and charges involved as rates higher than 1,000% APR are common
- You do not borrow more than you can repay or for longer than necessary. If you miss the repayment, the cost of borrowing even a small amount can become very high, very quickly

If consumers find themselves relying on payday loans regularly they may find it useful to re-examine their household budget.

Changes to payday loan regulation
On 1st April, 2014, the FCA (Financial Conduct Authority) took over regulation of the consumer credit market from the OFT (Office of Fair

Trading). One of the first things the FCA did was to crack down on lenders that offer 'High Cost Short Term Credit' (HCSTC), and this includes payday loans. The key changes include:

Limiting the number of times a loan can be rolled over

Currently if you can't afford to repay your payday loan on time you can usually roll it over to the next month. This flexibility comes as a cost and can quickly lead to a small short term loan turning into a hefty loan term debt.

Usually the balance of your loan is extended by a month, with extra interest and roll over fees whacked on to your borrowing. You generally only have to pay the interest charges upfront when you roll over a loan - but sometimes this can be rolled over as well.

Stopping lenders from trying to collect payment more than twice

Most payday lenders will use a CPA (Continuous Payment Authority) to collect payment. This is a way of taking money from your bank account that gives the lender the right to take payment on any date they like, and any amount they like. This is important because although lenders should let you know when they plan to take payment and how much it'll be, not all do.

CPAs can be a quick and flexible way to pay your bills as they help you avoid default and late payment charges if the lender tries to collect payment from your account and the money isn't there. However, there is growing concern that they are open to misuse, leading to payday lenders taking money from their customers' accounts without warning.

This causes problems if money is taken ahead of other bills, causing defaults on more important debts like your council tax, utilities, mortgage or rent; and leading to bank charges and future credit issues.

Under the new FCA rules, lenders will be limited to only two failed CPA attempts. This means that they can't continually try to withdraw money from your account when you don't have the funds available, and instead will need to contact you to find out what's going on. This limit can be reset if you decide to refinance or roll over your loan and pay the amount you currently owe.

Banning part payments by CPA

As well as introducing a limit on the number of times lenders can try to collect payment via CPA, they'll also be limited to how much they're able to collect.

In addition, caps will be introduced from 2nd january 2015 which will limit the amount of interest that can be charged. They are as follows:

- Initial cap of 0.8% a day in interest charges. Someone who takes out a loan of £100 over 30 days, and pays back on time, will therefore pay no more than £24 in interest
- A cap of £15 on the one-off default fee. Borrowers who fail to pay back on time can be charged a maximum of £15, plus a maximum of 0.8% a day in interest and fees
- Total cost cap of 100%. If a borrower defaults, the interest on the debt will build up, but he or she will never have to pay back more than twice the amount they borrowed

Personal loans

Shop around for the best value. Always consider how long it will take you to pay back the loan and how much you will pay in total, as well as how much your monthly payments are. Always check the Annual Percentage Rate (APR) being charged. It is the best way of comparing one deal with another. Generally, the lower the APR, the better the deal.

What to do if you have a complaint

Even if you think the goods are faulty, don't stop your payments or you could end up in trouble. See the shop manager at once and let your finance company know about the problem. If you can't sort it out yourself you should ask for advice from Consumerline on 0300 123 6262, your local Advice Centre or Citizens Advice.

****

Chapter. 7

Family Law-Children and Adults

_____

Parents Rights and obligations- Definition of a parent

The actual legal definition of a parent has been the subject of debate over the years. Whether the parent is a biological parent or psychological parent.

Biological parents

The law has traditionally approached the question of parentage by considering the biological link between adult and child as preferable. The law will rarely interfere with the authority of the biological parent, unless some other arrangement is preferable. In Re KD (a minor) (Ward: termination of access) 1988, Lord Templeman stated:

'The best person to bring up a child is the natural parent. It matters not whether the parent is wise or foolish, rich or poor, educated or illiterate, providing the child's moral and physical health is not endangered'.

There are two exceptions to this presumption: where the child is adopted (Adoption Act 1976 s39) and secondly where reproduction and childbirth follows on from sperm or egg donation (Human

119

Fertilisation and Embryology Act 2008). Adoption will terminate the legal (parental) responsibility of natural parents towards the child and also extinguishes any rights a parent may have over a child. Where a person donates genetic material (eggs, sperm, embryos) he relinquishes any rights of biological parentage in relation to any child that may be born as a result.

Psychological parents

Good parenting depends very much on the ability to form an emotional/psychological bond with a child. A strong attachment between parent and child is considered to be an indicator of a stable and emotionally healthy relationship.

This bond is not exclusive to the biological parent but can form with a number of people, such as foster and adoptive parents. The courts have recognised the possibility of the independence of the biological and psychological relationship.

Parenting and the changing social context

During the last 50 years or so the family has undergone significant changes with respect to public perception and also the law. A number of aspects of the family need to be considered: socially acquired parentage, sexual orientation and parentage and multi-cultural family arrangements. With regard to socially acquired parentage, this refers to step-parents, a situation which will arise through either divorce or one-parent families resulting in remarriage. It can be said that the step parent will acquire the mantle of mother or father, with their role far more significant than the actual biological absent parent.

With regard to sexual orientation, whilst the heterosexual family remains the norm, homosexual men will father children and lesbian women will give birth to babies. They would also be considered parents. The assumption that homosexuals are not fit parents was challenged in Re W (Adoption: Homosexual Adopter) 1997, in which Singer J held that there was nothing in the Adoption Regulations to prevent a homosexual adopting a child and allowed a 49 year old lesbian woman in a settled relationship to adopt. The Adoption and Children Act 2002 (see adoption) has now authorised adoption by homosexual men and women.

With regards to multi-cultural family arrangements, patterns of immigration over the last 50 years have changed the family make up of the United Kingdom. In addition, the cultural make up of the country has changed and with it a need by the law to recognise and accept different cultural traditions.

The legal parent

A parent, in the eyes of the law, is a person who has responsibility for a child. Parental responsibility means 'all the rights, duties, powers, responsibilities and authorities which by law a parent has in relation to the child and his property' (Children Act 1989 s3). Legal parenthood carries the right and responsibility to register a child's name within six months of its birth and apply for residence/contact orders, specific issue orders, change the child's name and to apply for a prohibited steps order to prevent the removal of the child from the country.

A parent is the natural mother or natural father of the child. However, not all fathers have parental responsibility for their child and other parties may also have parental responsibility for the child. In addition, the local authority may have parental responsibility for the child where the child is in care, and foster parents may have responsibility. More than one person can have parental responsibility for a child (CA 1989 s 2(5)). Where other parties have parental responsibility for the child, this will only last for the duration of the order made in their favour.

Surrogacy

The Surrogacy Arrangements Act 1985 is the main law governing surrogacy in the UK. The main principle is that if you use a surrogate they will be the legal mother of any child they carry. The Act prohibits commercial surrogacy arrangements. It received Royal Assent on 16 July 1985.

The Act came about as a response to the birth, on 4 January 1985, of Britain's first commercial surrogate baby amid a widespread public outcry.

The Act was amended by the Human Fertilisation and Embryology Act 1990 (so that surrogate mothers can always keep the baby if they change their mind) and the Human Fertilisation and Embryology Act 2008.

Mother's rights

The woman who gives birth is always treated as the mother in UK law and has the right to keep the child - even if they're not genetically related. However, parenthood can be transferred by parental order or adoption.

Surrogacy contracts are not enforced by UK law, even if you've a signed deal with your surrogate and have paid for her expenses. It's illegal to pay a surrogate in the UK, except for their reasonable expenses.

Father's rights

The child's legal father or 'second parent' will be the surrogate's husband or partner unless:

- legal rights are given to someone else through a parental order or adoption
- the surrogate's husband or civil partner did not give their permission to their wife or partner

If the surrogate has no partner, or they're unmarried and not in a civil partnership, the child will have no legal father or second parent unless the partner actively consents.

Become the child's legal parent

A person must apply for a parental order if you want to become the legal parent of the child.

Parental orders

A person must be genetically related to a child to apply for a parental order - in other words, be the egg or sperm donor - and must also be in a relationship where they and their partner are either:

- married
- civil partners
- living as partners

They and their partner must also:

- have the child living with them
- reside permanently in either the UK, Channel Islands or Isle of Man

A person cannot apply for a parental order if they are single.

See Re Z (A Child: Human Fertilisation and Embryology Act: Parental Order) [2015] EWFC 73 Application by a father for a parental order under section 54 (1) of the Human Fertilisation and Embryology Act 2008 solely in his favour. Application dismissed on the basis that such an order is not available to a sole parent.

How to apply

A person must fill in a 'C51 application form for a parental order' and give this to a family proceedings court within 6 months of the child's birth. They do not have to use their local family proceedings court, but they need to explain why if they do not. They need to provide the child's full birth certificate and will also be charged a court fee of £215 (as at 2020).

The court will then set a date for the hearing and issue a 'C52 acknowledgement form' that they must give to the child's legal parent, in other words, their surrogate.

The birth mother and anyone else who's a parent of the child must agree to the parental order by filling in form A101A.

A person cannot apply for a parental order once the child is older than 6 months.

Adoption

If neither a person or their partner are related to the child, or they are single, adoption is the only way they can become the child's legal parent.

Children born outside the UK

If the surrogate gives birth abroad, they can only apply for a parental order if they and their partner are living in the UK. The child will need a visa to enter the UK during this process. Using a surrogate abroad can be complicated because different countries have different rules.

Pay and leave

A person and their partner may be eligible for adoption pay and leave and paternity pay and leave if they use a surrogate. If they are not eligible for paid leave, they may be able to take parental leave or annual leave.

Surrogates

Every pregnant employee has the right to 52 weeks' maternity leave and to return to their job after this. What a birth mother does after the child is born has no impact on her right to maternity leave.

Parental responsibility

Any person who is a legal parent has parental responsibility. In accordance with the Children Act 1989, s2, more than one person may have responsibility for the child at any one time. Thus, parental responsibility is shared in the case of a married couple and is shared where parents are separated. In cases where children are taken into care, the natural parents will still have parental responsibility: the responsibility will simply be shared with foster parents.

The following outlines who has parental responsibility:

- The mother has automatic parental responsibility (whether a child is born within or out of marriage s 33 Human Fertilisation and Embryology Act 2008);
- The married father;

- The unmarried father has automatic responsibility if the Adoption and Children Act 2002 s111(2)(a)(c) applies;
- The unmarried father if he is granted a court order under the Children Act 1989, s4;
- The adoptive parents of an adoptive child;
- If a child is a ward of court the court stands in the position of parents and a court in wardship has parented responsibility;
- A guardian appointed by a parent by deed or will has parental responsibility after the parents death;
- The Children's Act 1989 created the institution of custodianship, under which many parental rights are given to the foster parent but some rights remain with the natural parent.

Proving parentage

In cases where the identity of the biological father is unknown and the mother wishes to establish parentage, or the child or father wishes to dispute parentage, an order for a declaration of paternity (under the Family Law Act) 1986, s55A, as amended by the Child Support, Pensions and Social Security Act 2000, s83(2) may be made. However, blood testing will only be ordered if it is considered to be in the child's best interests. In re O; Re J (children) (Blood Tests: Constraint) (2000) in two separate cases, a male applicant had obtained an order under s 20 (1) of the Family Law Reform Act 1969 for the use of blood tests designed to determine the paternity of a child who was the subject of the proceedings. In each case, the mother, whose consent was required under s 21(3) of the 1969 Act, refused to consent to the child's blood being tested. The court held that it was a matter for the mother to grant or withhold consent.

The courts, however, can order a blood test to be taken if it considers this to be in the best interests of child.

Step-parents

Where a parent remarries, the new spouse becomes the step-parent of any children of the previously married partner. Under the Adoption and Children's Act 2002, amending the Children's Act 1989 s 4(A)1:

Where a child's parent (A) who has parental responsibility for the child is married to a person who is not the child's parent (step parent) (a) parent A or, if the other parent of the child also has parental responsibility for the child, both parents may, by agreement with the step-parent provide for the step-parent to have parental responsibility for the child or (b) the court may, on application of the step-parent, order that the step-parent shall have parental responsibility for the child.

The Civil Partnership Act 2004 provides that civil partners will be eligible to apply for parental responsibility on the same basis as step parents.

Adoptive parents

An order of the court placing a child for adoption establishes the adoptive parent as the legal parent. The ACA 2002, s 46(1) states:

1) an adoption order is an order made by the court on an application under s 50 or 51 giving parental responsibility for a child to the adopters or adopter.

2) The making of an adoption order operates to extinguish the parental responsibility which any person other than the adopters or adopter has for the adopted child immediately before the making of the order.

Foster parents

When a child is in care of the local authority, he or she will be placed with foster carers. This can be a single adult or an adult couple in a family arrangement.

Parents and reproductive technology

The Human Fertilisation and Embryology Act 2008 came into effect on 13th November 2008 and amends the HFEA 1990.

The key provisions of the 2008 Act are to:

- Ensure that all human embryos outside the body-whatever the process used in their creation-are subject to regulation.
- Ensure regulation of "human-admixed" embryos created from a combination of human and animal genetic material for research.
- Ban sex-selection of offspring for non-medical reasons. Sex selection is allowed for medical reasons.
- Recognise same sex couples as legal parents of children conceived through the use of donated sperm, eggs or embryos.
- Retain a duty to take account of the welfare of the child in providing fertility treatment, but replace the reference to "the need for a father" with the "need for supportive parenting"- hence valuing the role of all parents.
- Alter the restrictions on the use of HFEA-collected data to help enable follow up research of infertility treatment.

Under the Human Fertilisation and Embryology Act (HFEA) 2008, where a person has donated sperm or eggs then he or she relinquishes any rights over the genetic material.

The HFEA determines the legal parent as a result of a child born from IVF treatment. The HFEA 2008, defines a 'mother' as 'the woman who is carrying or who has carried a child as a result of the placing in her of an embryo, or of sperm or eggs'.

Section 28 defines a father as being married to the woman 'at the time of placing in her of an embryo or the sperm or the eggs or of her insemination' unless it is shown that he did not consent to the placing in her of the embryo, sperm or eggs or to her insemination.

The Human Fertilisation and Embryology Authority (Disclosure of Donor) Regulations 2004

These regulations were passed to acknowledge a child's rights to know their genetic parentage. This is an important part of a child's identity. However, correspondingly, there is no obligation on the parents to tell the child that they were conceived using donated sperm.

Parties separating

When parties who consented to the placement of genetic material in the woman separate, a specific legal position arises. In the case of Re R (a child) (IVF Paternity of Child) 2005, the mother, A, and her partner B, were unmarried and sought IVF treatment which involved the fertilisation of A's eggs with sperm from a donor. In accordance with IVF procedure, B signed a form acknowledging that he would be the father of any child born in consequence. However, A nd B had already separated when implementation in A had taken place, about which B had no knowledge. On an application by B, the judge declared under HFEA 1990, s28(3) that B was the legal father of the resulting child.

The court of appeal allowed A's appeal. B appealed and the House of Lords dismissed the ruling of the court of appeal holding:

'that section 28(3) of the HFEA should only apply to cases falling clearly within it and the legal relationship of a parent should not be based on a fiction, especially where deception was involved: that the embryo had to have been placed in the woman when treatment services were provided for her and the man together; and that, although they had originally been so provided for A and B, they had not been when implementation took place'.

Parental responsibility and children's rights generally
Rights of Children in Domestic and International Law

The dominant statute governing the position of children in the UK is the Children Act 1989. This act sets out the fundamental premise of decisions taken in relation to children, which is the welfare principle. This provides that where decisions involving children are to be taken, the best interests of the children are the paramount consideration. The welfare principle has historically guided the development of children's law in the UK, and is the most significant restriction on children's autonomy and ability to exercise their rights independently. It is addressed in more detail below.

Further to the government's 'Every Child Matters' agenda, The Children's Act (CA) 2004 received royal assent in November 2004. The 2004 act codified 'five outcomes' for children, being their rights to:

- Be healthy

- Stay safe
- Enjoy and achieve
- Make a positive contribution
- Achieve economic well-being

The CA 2004 created a Children's Commissioner, and imposed enforceable duties on local authorities and other relevant bodies such as the police, NHS health services etc to work together in the provision of children's services. Every Children's Services Authority (local authority) is required to publish a Children and Young People's Plan. This plan should show how the authority intends to enable children in their area to meet the five outcomes, and must be regularly reviewed. The European Convention on Human Rights (ECHR) has been incorporated into UK law, and is relevant to the rights of children and young people in much the same way as it is to those of adults. In addition, where the ECHR rights of a competent child are infringed simply by reason of their being a child, the anti-discrimination provisions in Article 14 may be applicable.

The general function of the Office of the Children's Commissioner (OCC) is to promote the awareness of the views and the interests of children. The OCC is the only statutory body with a stated duty to have regard to the provisions of the UNCRC.

The OCC cannot undertake casework on behalf of children or investigate individual cases. However, it can act as a referral body for cases which fall within the remit of the Equality and Human Rights. The OCC has established a scheme to conduct 'child impact assessments' on proposed UK legislation. The aim of these assessments is be to provide an analysis of likely effect of the legislation on the rights and interests of children and young people. The weight that Parliament will give such assessments remains to be seen.

Key Areas of Parental Responsibility-Consultation with Children

Parents (and others exercising parental responsibility) are not legally obliged to consult their children as to their wishes or to involve them in decision making processes.

However, the exercise of parental responsibility is limited when children have sufficient understanding and capacity to make decisions about their own future. This was confirmed in the 1985 decision in Gillick v Wisbeach Health Authority, in which the House of Lords decided that a child under 16 could consent to medical treatment if he or she could understand what was involved in such treatment and was capable of expressing his or her views and wishes. This has come to be known as 'Gillick competence' and while the House of Lords did not identify a specific age at which children were to be deemed to be sufficiently mature to have their views considered, it follows from Gillick that the older the child, the greater the weight that will be attached to their views. This approach is consistent with certain provisions of the UNCRC – Article 5 which requires that children's rights be exercised in accordance with their evolving capacities and Article 12 which requires that in all decisions affecting children, due weight should be attached to their views.

In 2006 the High Court applying Gillick, confirmed that young people were entitled to confidential advice or treatment on sexual matters, which includes abortion, without the knowledge or consent of their parents. This position does not breach the child's parent's rights to private and family life under Article 8 ECHR.

Names

A child's parents have an unfettered right to name their child and are required by law to register the child's name within 42 days of the child's birth. Where only one person has parental responsibility that person can change the child's name (e.g by deed poll) without requiring the consent or permission of anyone else. Where there is more than one person with parental responsibility and dispute as to change of name then it will be necessary to seek the court's permission. The court will consider a range of factors but the paramount consideration will be the welfare of the child. The opinions of a older child are likely to be highly relevant. A change of name is considered to be serious step, relating as it does to a child's identity. Where a child becomes the subject of an adoption order, the adoptive parents acquire parental responsibility and have an absolute right to change a child's name.

With parental consent a child may use a different name from that on their birth certificate. A child of sixteen may change their name without their parent's consent. (A parent may apply to court in an attempt to prevent this but is unlikely to be successful). Equally, a child with sufficient maturity and understanding who is under the age of sixteen may apply to the court for permission.

Religion

A child who is sufficiently mature in accordance with the Gillick principles is entitled to choose his or her own religion. Where a dispute arises either between parents or between parents and the child over the choice of religious upbringing, the paramountcy of the child's welfare will prevail in resolving the conflict. If a parent seeks to impose a particular religion on a child it will not be tolerated if it causes harm to the child. Article 9 of the ECHR protects the right to freedom of thought, conscience and religion. (See also education, below).

Medical Treatment

In most cases it will be the parents who consent to medical treatment on behalf of their child. A child/young person can give valid consent provided the person providing treatment is of the view that he or she understands the nature and consequences of the treatment (ie that they are Gillick competent).

Children under 18 may also refuse medical treatment but under the wardship jurisdiction a court can order medical treatment, including termination of a pregnancy or sterilisation, if it is deemed necessary in the child's best interests. This power is most commonly used in cases where a young person refuses life saving medical treatment due as a consequence of an eating disorder or mental illness.

The ECHR has decided that compulsory medical treatment for the purposes of preventing death or serious injury does not amount to inhuman or degrading treatment contrary to Article 3 ECHR where a patient is not capable of giving consent.

Evans and Another v Alder Hey Children's NHS Foundation Trust and Another [2018] EWCA Civ 805

This is the case of a 23-month-old boy who died after spending more than a year in hospital which attracted widespread media attention. Alfie Evans's parents had been fighting to take the toddler to Rome for further treatment, but a court ruled his life support could be turned off several days ago.

Alfie was born to parents Tom Evans and Kate James, from Bootle in Merseyside, on 9 May 2016. He was first admitted to Alder Hey

Children's Hospital in Liverpool in December 2016 after suffering seizures and has been a patient in the hospital ever since.

Doctors diagnosed a degenerative neurological condition, which they have not been able to identify definitively. Alfie's parents and the hospital clashed over what should happen to Alfie, who had been in a semi-vegetative state for more than a year.

His parents said they wanted to fly him to a hospital in Italy but this was blocked by Alder Hey, which said continuing treatment was "not in Alfie's best interests".

The Alder Hey Children's Hospital NHS Foundation Trust went to the High Court to seek a declaration that "continued ventilator support is not in Alfie's best interests and in the circumstances it is not lawful that such treatment continue". Sitting at the High Court in Liverpool, Mr Justice Hayden began overseeing the case on 19 December.

Alder Hey said scans showed "catastrophic degradation of his brain tissue" and that further treatment was not only "futile" but also "unkind and inhumane". But his parents disagreed and wanted permission to fly him to the Bambino Gesu Hospital in Rome in the hope of prolonging his life. The Italian hospital, which has links to the Vatican, suggested operations to help Alfie breathe and keep him alive for an "undefined period". The judge said he would make a decision on what was best for Alfie if an agreement was not reached.

One of the dilemmas Alfie's case raised is whether doctors are the right people to determine if withdrawing life-support treatment is in "the best interests" of a terminally ill child. One of the key arguments presented by his parents was that they should decide what is best for their son. It was the same case made by the parents of Charlie Gard, the 11-month-old baby who died in 2017 following a similar battle over his treatment.

The law in the UK falls somewhere in-between. The 1989 Children's Act makes it clear that where a child is at risk of harm the state can and should intervene. This means that the rights of parents are not absolute and the state has been emboldened to challenge the view of parents where they believe a child's best interests are not being served. If a public body disagrees with the parents' choices, they must go to court in order to override this parental responsibility.

On 20 February, Mr Justice Hayden said doctors could stop providing life support for Alfie against his parents' wishes, saying the child required "peace, quiet and privacy". Mr Evans said he believed his son was still responsive, telling reporters outside court Alfie was "improving". But Michael Mylonas QC, representing the hospital, said: "One of the problems of this case is they [Alfie's parents] look at him and, barring the paraphernalia of breathing and feeding, he's a sweet, lovely, normal-looking boy who opens his eyes, [and] will smile..."

The hospital asserted that any movements by the child were "spontaneous seizures as a result of touching".

Mr Justice Hayden ruled in favour of hospital bosses and doctors were set to withdraw ventilation on 23 February before his parents embarked on a lengthy legal battle.

Alfie's parents refused to give up hope and took the case to the Court of Appeal on 6 March where judges upheld Mr Justice Hayden's decision. On 20 March, the couple appealed to the Supreme Court where justices refused to give the couple permission to mount another appeal. Despite this, their lawyers went to the European Court of Human Rights (ECHR) after exhausting all legal avenues in the UK. But three judges ruled the submission "inadmissible", saying they were unable to find any violation of human rights.

On 11 April, Mr Justice Hayden then endorsed an end-of-life care plan for Alfie, setting a date to switch off life support. This was the first time Alfie's parents were represented by the Christian Legal Centre (CLC) in court. The CLC is a sister body to Christian Concern and describes itself as an organisation that defends "individuals and churches who have suffered discrimination and challenges because of their desire to live and work according to biblical beliefs".

CLC lawyers began a final legal bid to the parents to take control over the treatment of their son on 16 April, claiming he was being "unlawfully detained". But this was rejected for a second time by the Court of Appeal and the Supreme Court. Two days later Mr Evans flew to Rome for a meeting with the Pope, pleading with him to "save our son".

Despite an urgent application to the ECHR on Monday, judges refused to intervene in the case, prompting angry scenes at Alder Hey Children's Hospital. Within hours, the Italian Ministry of Foreign Affairs granted 23-month-old Alfie Italian citizenship, hoping it would allow an "immediate transfer to Italy".

Pope Francis then tweeted his support for the family: "I renew my appeal that the suffering of his parents may be heard and that their desire to seek new forms of treatment may be granted." But this last-ditch appeal was dismissed by Mr Justice Hayden who stated that "Alfie is a British citizen" who "falls therefore under the jurisdiction of the High Court".

The Italian Embassy has since clarified it was not trying to challenge any decisions made previously by the British courts.

A spokesman described the granting of citizenship as a "signal" to the judge that should he change his mind, they are ready to facilitate his transfer to the Italian hospital.

A further hearing then took place on Tuesday afternoon in which Mr Hayden said the case had now reached its "final chapter". He rejected claims by Mr Evans's lawyers that his son was "significantly better" than first thought because he had been breathing unaided for 20 hours after doctors first withdrew life support.

Alfie's parents then launched a further appeal against the order stopping them from taking him to Italy, which was heard by a panel of three Court of Appeal judges, headed by Sir Andrew McFarlane. The judges upheld a ruling preventing the 23-month-old from travelling abroad after life support was withdrawn.

Consent to Marriage

Forcing someone to marry against their will is a criminal offence. Legislation introduced by the government is designed to help people in England and Wales. It also applies to UK nationals overseas who are at risk of becoming the victim of a forced marriage.

Forced marriage can involve physical, psychological, emotional, financial and sexual abuse including being held unlawfully captive, assaulted and raped. The maximum penalty for the offence of forced marriage is seven years imprisonment. Law enforcement agencies will also be able to pursue perpetrators in other countries where a UK national is involved under new powers defined in legislation.

A marriage where one party is under 16 is void. Young people between 16 and 18 may marry with parental consent. If the parents are separated or divorced the consent of both parents is necessary and if the child is in the care of the local authority it is necessary to obtain the consent of all persons having parental responsibility for the child.

Article 12 of the Convention protects the right of men and women of 'marriageable age' to marry. The prohibition on the marriage of children under 16 years does not infringe the right to marry because Article 12 clearly permits states to regulate the age at which a person is able to marry. Similarly, it is not possible to enter into a civil partnership if under the age of 16. A young person of 16 or 17 may only register a civil partnership with the consent of their parents.

Corporal Punishment

In international law physical punishment of children is totally prohibited. However, in the UK parents still have the right to administer reasonable physical chastisement to a child. It is possible to defend a charge of common assault against a child on the basis that the force used was no more than reasonable punishment. This position has been strongly criticised by the UN Committee, and by the Children's Commissioners for England, Wales, Scotland and Northern Ireland, who in 2006 issued a joint statement condemning the UK's position and calling for an outright ban on the physical punishment of children. Corporal punishment is prohibited as a form of punishment in all other circumstances including as a punishment following conviction for an offence, in education and in care or foster homes.

In 2005 the UK House of Lords held that the ban on corporal punishment in independent schools did not amount to a breach of the parents' rights under Articles 8 and 9 ECHR. Parliament was bound to respect a religious belief in corporal punishment in school, but entitled to legislate in children's best interests against the manifestation of that belief.

Leaving Home

Generally, young people under 16 cannot leave home unless their parents agree.. The law relating to 16 to 17 year olds is not clear but it appears that they probably can leave home without parental consent. In theory, parents can apply to court for the return home of a child under 18 by seeking an injunction in wardship proceedings or a residence order. However, a court is extremely unlikely to order a child of 16 to 17 to return home against his or her wishes.

A court may make a residence order in favour of another adult if this is deemed to be in the child's best interests. This can be done on the adult's application or by the child if he or she is deemed to have sufficient understanding. The leave of the court is required,

Police will return a runaway child under 16 to his or her parents or to the local authority if he or she is in care unless they have reasonable cause to believe the child is in danger or at risk. In such circumstances the police may hold the child in police protection. The police then liaise with social services as to whether further action should be taken to protect the child. The police are unlikely to return a child over the age of 16 to his or her parents.

Ages of Consent

The legal definition of childhood remains quite fluid, and while children do not acquire full independence until they reach the age of 18 they can legally engage in certain adult activities before that age.

At 16 a young person can consent to sex, join the armed services (although they will not generally be deployed on active service until they are 18) and get married with their parent's consent. Whereas 16 year olds have traditionally been able to buy cigarettes, in October 2007 the minimum age rose to 18.

The Children Act 1989 aims to encourage parents to agree about the child's welfare in the event of separation or divorce by providing for the continuation of parental responsibility for divorced parents and by requiring the courts to refrain from making orders unless they are desirable in the child's best interests (the 'no order' principle). This approach is reinforced by the development of conciliation and mediation processes to assist parents to reach agreement.

Where there is agreement between parents they are not required to attend court in divorce proceedings in relation to the children. The court must simply be satisfied that appropriate arrangements have been made for children having received a written declaration to that effect and the divorce is granted. In cases where the court is concerned about the plans for the children it can order a welfare report but this power is very rarely used. However it is concerning that in an uncontested case there is no formal way in which children can express their views if they wish to do so.

In 2001 the Children and Family Court Advisory and Support Service (CAFCASS) was established. CAFCASS has a number of functions. In this context the most important is the provision of Child and Family Reporter to carry out conciliation and reporting functions in disputes between parents over residence and contact.

Parents making applications for residence or contact with a child may be required to attend a conciliation appointment with a mediator or child and family reporter. The purpose of the conciliation stage is to assist the parties to resolve their disputes. If this is not possible then the Court may order a report to be prepared on the matter of residence or contact. A child and family reporter involved at the conciliation plays no further part in the process and does not participate in the preparation of any reports for the court.

In addition to applications for residence and contact, which are made under section 8 of the Children Act 1989, parents can also apply for a specific issue order requiring a particular action by another parent or for a prohibited steps order to prevent a parent from taking certain steps, for example removing a child from the other parents care and control. Section 8 applications often involve the use of child and family reporters to provide the court with an objective assessment of what is in the child's best interests. Children and young people may apply to court for section 8 orders provided they can demonstrate sufficient maturity and understanding. However, the court does not have to grant a child leave, and retains a discretion to refuse an application of a competent child. (see chapter 11 for more on different order).

Welfare Principle The concept of welfare is not defined in the Children Act 1989 but the following factors which constitute the 'welfare checklist' are used to assist the Court in its determination:

- The ascertainable wishes and feelings of the child – in light of his or her age and understanding;
- The physical, emotional and educational needs of the child;
- The likely effect of any change on the child's circumstances;
- The age, sex, background and any other characteristics which the court considers to be relevant;
- Any harm which the child has suffered or is at risk of suffering;
- How capable the child's parents (and/or any other relevant person) are of meeting the child's needs; and
- The range of powers available to the court.

The child and family reporter is also required to take the welfare checklist into account in the preparation of his or her report.

Article 8 of the ECHR – the right to respect for family life – impacts on this decision making process in that a court must be aware of the parents' right to respect for their family life. The courts have taken the view that while a balance must be struck between the competing interests of parents and children, the welfare principle continues to predominate under the Children Act 1989.

In most cases such children will not participate directly but will be represented by a children's guardian appointed by CAFCASS. Most children's guardians have worked as social workers but they are appointed to act independently and to represent the child's interests.

Contact Disputes

The question of how much contact a child should have with a non-residential parent is a difficult matter for the court to resolve to the satisfaction of the parents and the child. Under the Children Act 1989 contact is expressed as a right of the child although the ECHR has recognised it as an element of a parent's family life. In striking a balance between the competing interests the courts are guided by considerations of the child's welfare as the paramount consideration but the view in the vast majority of cases is that maintaining a relationship with both parents is in the child's best interests. Terminating direct contact between a child and a non residential parent is a rare occurrence and usually only happens where there has been violence or abuse of an extreme nature or where for other reasons the child does not wish to continue to have a relationship with his or her parents.

Children and the Criminal Justice system

More recently, the Children and Adoption Act 2006 has given the courts greater powers to enforce orders for contact.

The principal aim of the youth justice system is to prevent offending by children and young persons. The CDA seeks to achieve this aim by promoting a range of diversionary tactics which remove children from the criminal justice system and introducing a range of alternative sentences if children are thought to be acting in an anti social manner. The use of such measures however is controversial because they effectively create status offences where behaviour which would not attract criminal sentences if it were committed by adults is criminalised in respect of children.

Criminal Responsibility

Children below the age of ten cannot be charged with criminal offences as they are considered incapable of committing criminal offences. This is considerably lower than the age in most other countries and in both 1995 and 2002 the UN Committee recommended that the age of criminal responsibility be raised. Under the CDA, children under the age of ten can be the subject of a Child Safety Order. The order has the effect of placing the child under the supervision of a social worker or the youth offending team and it may require a child to comply with certain conditions such as curfews.

Another new measure introduced by the CDA (amended by the Policing and Crime Act 2009) was the introduction of Local Curfew Schemes which allow the Local Authority in consultation with the Home Office to introduce a scheme whereby children are banned from being in a public place during certain hours unless they are accompanied by an adult. Police can take a child home and inform the local authority if they are of the view that the child breached the order. The local authority has an obligation to follow up on any breach by making its own enquiries. This scheme was originally intended to apply to children under ten but can now be used for older children as well.

A further initiative of the CDA was the Anti Social Behaviour Order (ASBO) which could be used on any person over the age of ten years. ASBO's have now been replaced by Community Protection Notice (CPN) or Criminal Behaviour Orders (CBO) plus Civil Injunctions. The local authority or the police can make an application to a Magistrates' Court for a CPN or CBO where it appears that a person or family is behaving in a manner which has caused or is likely to cause harassment, alarm or distress to a person or people not of the same household. This is a civil application and the onus is on the defendant to disprove the allegations. These orders can last up to two years and a breach of an order is a criminal offence. A CBO or Civil injuction are issued to children 10 or over and a CPN 16 or over.

In 2005 the CDA was amended to allow Parental Compensation Orders to be granted in relation to the behaviour of children under the age of 10 (there is no minimum age). Under these measures a parent can be fined up to £5,000 for the behaviour of their children.

The CDA also removed the concept of 'doli incapax' under which children between the ages of ten to 13 were deemed incapable of knowing the difference between right and wrong. These children are now treated the same as other young people aged 14 to 17 years.

The rules for police questioning, search and detention of young people are the same as for adults but young people have additional rights. Parents must be informed of the arrest and detention and interviews should only take place in the presence of an appropriate adult. The appropriate adult can be a parent, guardian, social worker or other responsible adult aged at least 18. The role of the appropriate adult is unclear but they should be able to advise and assist the juvenile and to ensure the interview is conducted fairly.

When it is a first offence the police have the discretion to issue a reprimand instead of proceeding with prosecution. For a second offence a warning may be used. A second warning may only be issued if the latest offence is not serious and more than two years have elapsed since the making of the first warning. Reprimands and warnings can only be given if the young person admits the offence, has no previous convictions and it is considered contrary to the public interest for the offender to be prosecuted. Reprimands and warnings are made at the police station in the presence of the appropriate adult. Following a warning the young person is referred to the Youth Offending Team for an assessment to decide whether a rehabilitation programme is appropriate. Reprimands and warnings do not form part of a person's criminal record although they may be brought if there are court proceedings in the future.

Criminal trials

The majority of young people are tried in Youth Court. This is a specialist branch of the Magistrate's Court. Certain serious offences such as murder, manslaughter, rape, arson, aggravated burglary and robbery are heard in the Crown Court. In both courts there is a requirement that the welfare of the child is considered when sentencing but this is a weaker requirement than in the family courts. Following a decision of the ECHR guidance was issued to remind judges of the importance of guaranteeing the fair trial rights of young people in accordance with Article 6. In particular they are required to ensure that children sit with their lawyers and understand the nature of the proceedings and the evidence which is being given against them. In addition judges are required to provide regular breaks and to restrict reporting in the media where appropriate.

Sentencing--Community sentences

In common with adults, young people may be subject to a range of sentences including a fine, attendance order or supervision order. Supervision orders may include a range of conditions such as participation in particular activities, night restrictions or a requirement that the child lives in social services accommodation for up to 6 months. New sentences under the CDA include reparation orders and action plan orders. These are intended to provide young people with the opportunity to avoid custodial sentences and to make amends to victims or to the community.

Referral orders are similar and were introduced by the Criminal Justice and Youth Evidence Act 1999 (and are now provided for in the Powers of Criminal Courts (Sentencing) Act 2000. The are aimed at the first time offender who admits the offence and where the offence would only normally attract a fine. It allows the juvenile to be referred to the Youth Offending team and work is carried out to challenge their behaviour.

Children in Detention-Custodial Sentence

The CDA introduced the detention and training order for young people between the ages of 12 and 17 years. The sentence is intended to be divided between a custodial stage and a training stage. It is available for 15 to 17 year olds if they are convicted of an offence which is so serious that only custody is appropriate and they are persistent offenders, or for 12 to 14 year olds who are convicted of a serious offence and the court is of the view that custody is appropriate and again they are persistent offenders. It can also be available for 11 to 12 year olds if made available by the Home Secretary where the child is found to be a persistent offender and custody is deemed necessary to protect the public. The training half of the sentence is supervised and it is intended to provide skills aimed at rehabilitation. This sentence can be made for 24 months provided that it does not exceed the adult sentence available for the offence.

Detention at Her Majesty's Pleasure

Young offenders convicted under the age of 18 of murder may be detained at Her Majesty's pleasure which is indefinite detention firstly in social services secure accommodation transferring at 18 to a young offender institution and at 21 to prison. The length of detention is however set by the Lord Chief Justice and it is for the Parole Board to determine whether the young person should be released.

Detention under section 53 of the Children and Young Person Act 1933 as modified by The Children and Young Persons Act 2008.

Young offenders under the age of 18 convicted of grave crimes which would attract a period of imprisonment of 14 years or more if committed by an adult may be convicted to a period of detention for periods in excess of 24 months provided that the sentence does not exceed the maximum term which would be imposed if an adult committed the offence. The court should determine the appropriate sentence for rehabilitation and deterrence and for young people this is normally one half of the sentence before referral is made to the parole board. Young people are referred to the Parole Board for a determination as to whether it is safe to release the young person on licence once the tariff period has expired.

Conditions of Detention

The UK government ratified the UNCRC with a reservation in relation to Article 37 (that wherever it is necessary for children to be detained, they should be held separately from adults). While progress in this area has been made, the UK retains this reservation and increasing prison numbers may mean that children are again detained in adult facilities.

In 2006 the Carlile Inquiry reported on the routine use of strip-searching, restraint and segregation against children in custody. The report called for greater safeguards for children in custody and stated that may of the practices would be regarded as child abuse in any other setting. In particular, the use of painful 'distraction' techniques may raise issues under Articles 3 and 8 of the ECHR.

In a recent decision (2007) the High Court has confirmed the existence of a duty on Social Services departments to assess the needs of detained children where there is a real prospect of their release from detention.

Education

While education is recognised as a right of the child, international and domestic human rights laws have tended to focus disproportionately on the rights of parents to control the content of their children's education. For example, Article 2, Protocol 1 of the Convention states that everyone has a right to education and then goes on to say that the State has an obligation to respect the rights of parents to ensure that education and teaching of their children is in conformity with the parents' religious and philosophical convictions. The emphasis on the rights of parents as consumers in education law and policy is problematic because it dilutes the child's right to an education and it discourages acceptance of children's right to participate. The Joint Committee on Human Rights has expressed concerns about the inadequacy of recent education legislation, in light of Article 12 UNCRC.

The law governing education in England and Wales is complex not least because there is a range of different types of state maintained schools, independent (albeit state funded) schools such as Academies and City Technology Colleges, and fully independent schools . Further, the Education and Inspections Act 2006 allowed schools to become Trust (foundation) schools.

Compulsory education

Children over the age of five and under the age of 16 are of compulsory education age and they must receive full time education. Parents are required to ensure that a child receives efficient full-time education suitable to his or her age, ability and aptitude and to ensure that any special educational needs are met by attendance at school or otherwise. Parents may educate children at home or engage a private tutor, but the Local Education Authority (LEA) must be satisfied that the education is of a sufficiently high standard. If the LEA are concerned that a child is not receiving a suitable education other than at school they may serve formal notice on the parents requiring them to satisfy the LEA otherwise. Where the parents fail to do so, the LEA can serve a School Attendance Order (SAO) requiring the parents to register the child at a named school. Parents must be given notice of the LEA's intention to serve this order and the named school must not be one from which the child has been excluded. The relevant legislation comes from section 437-444 of the Education Act 1996. Government Guidelines on Home Education state: 'A school attendance order should be served after all reasonable steps have been taken to try to resolve the situation.

The SAO lasts while the child is of compulsory school age unless it is repealed by a court order. Where a parent fails to comply with the SAO s/he can be prosecuted before a Magistrates' Court and can be fined up to £1000. Where a parent knows that a child is not attending school and fails to take steps to make the child attend, the parent can be fined up to £2500 or imprisoned for not more than three months. A court which has convicted a parent for a failure to comply with a SAO can direct the LEA to apply for an Education Supervision Order. The LEA does not have to do this but it must tell the court why it has chosen not to make an application.

The purpose of an Education Supervision Order is to guide parents and children to ensure that the children receive a satisfactory education. The Department of Health has issued guidance on the use of Education Supervision Orders which last for up to one year initially, but may be extended for up to three years at a time. They cannot last beyond the point at which the child is no longer of compulsory school age.

Special Educational Needs

LEA's must make special provision for children who have learning disabilities to ensure that they are provided with education which meets their needs. The general preference is that children with special educational needs (SEN) remain in mainstream schools.

Schools have an obligation to ensure that a child's special educational needs are identified and known to those involved in teaching the child. This process is done by way of assessment and a child who has SEN is 'statemented' – a statement of the child's needs and measures which are to be taken to deal with those needs is provided. If parents are not satisfied with the eventual provisions or the nominated school, they may appeal to a Special Educational Needs Tribunal provided that they require the assessment of the child themselves. The question of whether a child requires assessment and statementing can often be contentious in that parents may wish to have a child statemented but can encounter considerable difficulties in convincing a school to undertake this process.

Where the school refuses to statement a child the parents can appeal to the SEN tribunal. Each school is required to have a Special Education Needs Co-ordinator (SENCO) who is responsible for overseeing the provision of SEN for a child within the school.

Parenting Contracts and Orders

An LEA or school governing body can apply to the magistrates' court for a parenting order covering the parents of a child who has been excluded from school. The relevant exclusion must have been either permanent or for two fixed periods within twelve months. A parenting order requires the parent to exercise control over the child, and to attend counselling or a guidance programme. Parents who fail to keep to the terms of a parenting order are guilty of a criminal offence, and could be fined.

Parenting contracts are a provision allowing for formal agreements between parents and the school or LEA, which codify the intended action in relation to a specific child's attendance and behaviour.

Employment

No one under 16 can legally be employed in work other than light work, or undertake any work which is likely to be harmful to their safety, health, development, or that will affect their attendance at school or participation in work experience. Children under the age of 14 can only be employed in specific areas.

Specific rules in any given area will be governed by local authority by-laws. Employers who want to employ children or young people under school leaving age are required to get a permit from their local authority. The permit must be signed by both the employer and one of the child's parents. There are strict rules as to how many hours a young person under 16 can legally work. A person of compulsory school age must not work more than two hours on a school day, or more than twelve hours in any week when s/he is attending school.

Under 16 year olds are not entitled to the National Minimum Wage, nor to paid holiday. For the different rates of the NMW go to https://www.gov.uk/national-minimum-wage-rates.

Performance licences and supervision for children

A child may need a licence if they're under school leaving age and taking part in:

- films, plays, concerts or other public performances that the audience pays to see, or that take place on licensed premises
- any sporting events or modelling assignments where the child is paid

The person in charge of running the event must apply to the child's local council for a child performance licence.

Travelling and Leaving the Country

Since October 1998 all children who were not on a valid 10-year passport need to have a passport of their own to travel abroad. A parent or other person with a residence order may take a child out of the country for a period of four weeks without the permission of non-residential parents or other holders of parental responsibility. This is to allow parents to take their children for holidays without requiring permission of the other parent. However where a parent is concerned about the frequency of such trips or has fears that a parent may abduct a child he or she can apply to the court to impose restrictions on removal or require that a passport be surrendered.

Removal of a child from the jurisdiction on a more permanent basis is more complicated. Again the paramountcy of the child's welfare will prevail in considering whether such a move should be permitted. A court will also consider the impact of the removal on the child's relationship with his or her other parent and any siblings or extended family members who are to remain in the UK.

Where a child is removed from the jurisdiction without agreement it is possible to use the Hague Conventions on Child Abduction (the Hague Conventions), which provide a procedure for the summary return of abducted children. The aim is that the law of the country of habitual residence of the child should be enforced unless specific and somewhat restrictive grounds can be satisfied that the courts in the country of habitual residence should sort out any difficulties that need resolution. While courts must take into account the wishes and feelings of the child, children do not have a right to invoke the Hague Conventions in their own right.

Access to Justice and Redress

A Gillick competent child is entitled to instruct a solicitor in their own right. Where public funding (legal aid) is available a child will be entitled to make an application for such funding in the same way as an adult. Where the child is under 16 the Legal Aid Agency will normally expect an application on behalf of a child to be made by an adult acting on the child's behalf. If there are no suitable adults an application can be made by the child in person.

A child will be the appropriate applicant for legal aid where the legal problem relates to them and/or they have standing to bring an action. In certain areas, where an appeal right vests in a child's parent (such a school admission appeals) the Legal Aid Agency will not view a child as an appropriate applicant for funding, notwithstanding that their rights are affected.

An action under the Human Rights Act 1998 can only be brought by a victim or would-be victim of the alleged violation. Where a child is the victim of an alleged HRA breach, a parent will not have standing to bring the action and a child should not be refused funding on the basis that an adult could fund/bring the action in their place.

On a child's application for public funding it is their own means that will be taken into account. All applications, be subject to a consideration as to whether there are alternative sources of funding available; this could include consideration of a child's parent's financial circumstances, and a judgement may be made that it would be reasonable for a parent/guardian to seek advice and/or bring any action in their own name, rather than through the child.

The Civil Procedure Rules require a child to conduct proceedings through a litigation friend. However a child can apply to the court for an order that they be allowed to conduct proceedings without a litigation friend (CPR part 21).

For information on Legal Aid and the legal system generally in Scotland go to:

www.mygov.scot/legal-aid
For Northern Ireland:
www.nidirect.gov.uk/articles/legal-aid-schemes

****

Chapter.8

The Law and Divorce or Dissolution

Divorce law generally

I will deal with the (slight differences) between heterosexual couples and same-sex couples when it comes to ending a marriage or civil partnership at the end of the chapter. Most of the law, and the subsequent financial and child related issues affecting divorce, dissolution of Civil partnerships or Same-sex marriages is similar and applies to both.

Divorce law has developed over the years through legislation made by Parliament and through the build up of "precedents" or through cases decided by the courts. However, in the last thirty years there have been fundamental changes in the way society, and the law, has come to view divorce.

Modern divorce law recognizes that "irretrievable breakdown" of a marriage should be the one and only ground for divorce. This recognition signalled a move away from the idea of "guilty parties" in divorce. At present (2020) a Bill has been presented to Parliament, The Divorce, Dissolution and Separation Bill which is destined to become law. This will make the whole process of divorce that much easier, although, not surprisingly, the Bill has its opponents.

Before the introduction of the notion of irretrievable breakdown it was held that one party had to prove that the other party was guilty of destroying the marriage before divorce could be granted. The law is now much more flexible in its recognition of the breakdown of a marriage.

Since the present law was introduced, making it much easier to obtain divorce, the number of marriage breakdowns in Britain has risen significantly, with one in three couples filing for divorce. This is currently the highest rate in Europe.

There are a lot of problems associated with the law, and the role of those who make divorce law generally. The whole question of divorce law is under scrutiny, particularly the question of whether or not the law should attempt to keep marriages intact or whether it should seek to ease the transition to final separation without presenting unnecessary obstacles. However, although we hear periodic announcements from different politicians on the importance of keeping the family unit intact, and by implication making it harder for people to divorce, the whole climate has changed over the years whereby the law seems to be the facilitator of divorce as opposed to dictating whether or not people can get a divorce.

There has also been a major shift in the law concerning children of divorcing couples. Under The Children Act 1989 (as amended), parents in divorce proceedings are encouraged to take the initiative and take matters into their own hands, making their own decisions concerning the child's future life after divorce. The courts role has been greatly restricted. (See chapter 4)

The Child Support Act 1991 (as amended by the 1995 CSA) has also dramatically changed the role of the courts in divorce proceedings. The Child Maintenance Service, assesses and determines applications for maintenance in accordance with a set formula (see chapter 5) The courts will only now deal with applications for maintenance in certain circumstances.

Law generally – the courts

Before looking at the law surrounding divorce in greater depth, we should look briefly at the structure of the courts and how divorce law is administered.

County courts

Most divorces are handled by a branch of the county court system known as the divorce county courts.

County courts are local courts, usually found within towns and cities throughout England and Wales. These courts do not deal with criminal matters but they attempt to find solutions to virtually every other type of problem facing people in every day life. Such problems might be those that arise between businesses and their customers, between neighbours and between landlord and tenant, to name but a few. Decisions concerning divorce cases, and subsequent orders, were made by Judges and District Judges. However, since 2017, and a reorganisation of the Divorce Courts, a centralisation has meant that 47 Regional Courts were reduced to just 11 divorce centres. Most uncontested decree nisi applications are now considered by legal advisors rather than district judges. This has led, inevitably, in a slowdown and one criticism is that divorces, particularly 'quickie' divorces are taking longer to finalise.

In addition to the judges and legal advisors there is also a large staff of officials who provide the administrative machinery of the courts. Like all administrators, they are the backbone of the operation.

The High Court

Sometimes, rarely, divorce cases need to be referred to the High Court. There are several sections of the high court-the section responsible for divorce and other similar matters is known as the Family Division. However, the majority of divorce cases will be heard in the county courts.

Hearing your divorce case

Hearings related to divorce cases are either in "Open" court or in "Chambers". Proceedings in open court are heard in the court-room itself. They are usually formal and members of the public are allowed to attend. However, most divorces are heard in chambers. These proceedings are private and the general public has no right to attend or listen. Only those people directly concerned with the case are allowed to attend.

Same sex couples-grounds for divorce

For the most part, the grounds for divorce in same sex marriages are the same, but, as stated, a same sex marriage cannot rely on adultery because the definition of adultery is 'engaging in sexual intercourse with a person of the opposite sex.

Therefore if a gay couple separated because one of them went off with a member of the same sex, they could not rely on adultery – it would have to be 'unreasonable behaviour'."

Generally

The first question facing couples that wish to divorce is whether or not they qualify at the outset to bring proceedings, i.e., what are the

160

ground rules. If one or other parties wishes to file for divorce, the most basic requirement that must be fulfilled is that they should have been married for one-year minimum. They must also be "domiciled" in this country. Both parties must have their permanent homes in England or Wales when the petition is started or both parties should be living in either England or Wales when the petition is started. If this is not the case then both parties must have had their last home in England or Wales when the petition is started or must have been living in England or Wales for at least a year on the day the petition is started. There are a few other stipulations concerning domicile. Leaflet D183 which can be found on the www.justice.gov.uk website explains domicile in depth.

A court can halt proceedings for divorce in England if it would be better for the case to be heard in another country. Usually, the court would try to decide which country is the most appropriate, or with which country the divorcing couple are most closely associated.

Grounds for divorce – the 'five facts'.

As we have seen, currently there is only one ground for granting a divorce, that is the irretrievable breakdown of marriage. Fundamentally, this means that your marriage has broken down to such a degree that it cannot be retrieved and the only solution is to end it legally. (Matrimonial Causes Act 1973). The person, or spouse, who requests a divorce is known as the "petitioner". the other party is known as the "respondent".

Although there is only one ground for divorce, the court has to be satisfied that there is clear evidence of one of the following five facts:

1. that the respondent has committed adultery and the petitioner cannot, or finds it intolerable, to live with the respondent;

2. that the respondent has behaved in such a way that you cannot reasonably be expected to live with him or her (unreasonable behaviour)

3. that the respondent has deserted you for a continuous period of two years immediately before the presentation of your petition for divorce.

4. that parties to a marriage have lived apart for more than two years prior to filing for divorce and that there is no objection or defence to filing for divorce. This is known as the "no fault" ground;

5. that parties to marriage have lived apart continuously five years prior to filing for divorce.

We should now look at each of these "five facts" in more depth.

1. Adultery

Quite simply, adultery is defined as heterosexual sex between one party to a marriage and someone else.

Adultery usually means that a "full" sexual act has been committed so therefore if there has not been penetration then this will not be seen to be adulterous.

For adultery to be proved, an admission by the respondent or evidence of adultery is usually sufficient. The co-respondent need not be named in the divorce petition. If you do mention the name of the co-respondent involved in the adultery, that person is entitled to take part in the divorce proceedings in so far as they affect them. The court will provide the co-respondent with copies of all the relevant divorce papers and he or she will have the opportunity to confirm or deny anything said about him or her in the divorce proceedings. Proving adultery is the first step. You then have to satisfy the courts that you find it intolerable to live with the respondent any further. However, it

162

is not essential to prove that you find it intolerable to live with the respondent because of their adultery. It may be that your marriage has been unhappy for some time and that the adulterous act has proven to be the end. If, after you discover the respondent's adultery, you continue to live together as man and wife for a period of six months or more, you will not be able to rely on adultery as a reason for divorce. As long as the periods of living together after the adultery do not exceed six months in total, the courts will completely disregard them. This gives some room for attempts at reconciliation.

2. Unreasonable behaviour

Although "unreasonable behaviour" is a commonly cited fact for divorce, in practice the court has stringent criteria, which must be met before this is accepted. The law actually says that you must demonstrate that your spouse has behaved in such a way that you cannot reasonably be expected to continue to live with that person.

The court considering your case will look at the particular circumstances surrounding your situation and will then decide whether or not you should continue to tolerate your partner's behaviour within marriage.

The main principle underlying unreasonable behaviour is that it is particular to your own situation and that it cannot be seen as relative to other people's behaviour.

You must prove that the behaviour of your partner has gone well beyond the kind of day-to-day irritations that many people suffer and there is real reason to grant a divorce.

Examples of such behaviour range from continuous violence and threatening or intimidating behaviour, drunkenness, sexual

163

perversions, neglect, and imposing unreasonable restrictions on another person.

3. Desertion

The fact that you must prove that your spouse has deserted you for a continuous period of two years can present difficulties.

If you are seeking a divorce on the basis of desertion, then it is likely that you will need to employ a solicitor who will need to check rigorously that you comply with the (often complex) requirements upon which a court will insist before granting a divorce. In the main, desertion has arisen because of other associated problems within marriage, and therefore this factor can often be joined with others when applying for a divorce

The simplest form of desertion is when one person walks out on another for no apparent reason. Desertion, however, is not just a physical separation of husband and wife. It implies that the deserting party has rejected all the normal obligations associated with marriage.

Before desertion is proven a court will need to be satisfied of two things:

1. You must demonstrate that you and your spouse have been living separately for a continuous period of two years immediately before you started the divorce proceedings. Although it is usual for separation to start when one person leaves the marital home, it can also happen whilst you are living under the same roof, but living totally separate lives.

The courts are very rigorous indeed when determining that this is the case and will need to be satisfied that your lives are indeed separate and that you can no longer go on carrying out functions jointly. The court will disregard short periods during the separation where you may have attempted to patch up your differences. However, for example, if you attempt to reconcile six months into the initial two year period and this lasts for two months before you separate again, although the courts will not make you start again they will make you wait a further two months before they will hear your divorce. Therefore, the two years becomes two years and two months.

2. That your spouse has decided that your marriage is over-you must also be able to demonstrate that when he or she stopped living with you, your spouse viewed the marriage as ended and intended to separate from you on a permanent basis. You will not be able to claim desertion if you consented to the separation. The court will take consent to mean that you made it clear from the outset that you consented to separation, through your words or actions.

In addition, you will not be able to claim desertion if your spouse had perfectly good reason to leave, for example he or she may have gone abroad with your full knowledge, to work or may have entered hospital for a long period.

If your spouse leaves because of your own unreasonable behaviour, then you cannot claim desertion. If you are to blame in this case, the courts will not accept desertion.

Finally, because the courts see desertion as essentially separation against your will, then if you come back together again on a permanent basis you can no longer claim desertion.

4. Separation for two years with consent

As with desertion, the particular circumstances in which the law looks upon you as having been separated for two years can include periods of time where you may have been under the same roof together but not functioning as a married couple. There may be short periods during this time where you have lived together, for example, an attempt at reconciliation.

However, as with desertion you will not be able to count these periods towards the two years separation. Therefore, if you have a trial reconciliation period for three months then you will have to wait two years and three months before you can apply for divorce.

The fundamental difference between desertion and separation with consent is that you would not be granted a divorce on the basis of separation if your spouse did not give his or her consent to the divorce.

The court has rigid criteria for proving that your spouse consents to the divorce. Consent is only seen as valid if your spouse has freely given it without pressure. There must also be full understanding on his or her part of what a divorce will mean and how it will affect his or her life.

The court sends a form to divorcing parties soon after initial divorce papers are filed, together with explanatory notes and it is at this point when your spouse will give consent. If your spouse will not consent to divorce and you cannot prove either desertion or adultery then you will be in the position where you will have to wait until five years separation has elapsed before you can seek a divorce. In relation to the above, i.e., divorces granted on the basis of two years separation and consent or five years separation, the courts can exercise special powers to ensure that the financial and personal position of the respondent is protected. The courts can sometimes delay the process of divorce, or even prevent it, to make sure that there is no undue suffering or exploitation.

5. Five years separation

The final of the "five facts" is the fact of five years separation. If you have been separated for five or more years the courts will grant a divorce whether or not the other party agrees to it, subject to what has been said above. Again, the courts will allow for a period of attempted reconciliation up to six months and the same rules concerning length of time apply as with the other facts. Should you live together for longer than six months, the courts will demand that you start the five-year period again.

Reconciliation

As been shown, in all the provisions of the law relating to each of the five facts which have to be demonstrated in addition to the main ground of "irretrievable breakdown", there are built in provisions for reconciliation. The law is fairly flexible when taking into account attempts at reconciling and sorting out differences.

In effect, these built in provisions allow for a period of up to six months in which both parties can make a concerted attempt at solving their problems. If these attempts are unsuccessful then their legal position vis-a-vis divorce proceedings will not be jeopardized. The reconciliation provisions apply for a period up to six months or separate periods not exceeding six months.

In addition to this, a solicitor, if you have one, will need to certify that he or she has discussed the possibility of reconciliation with you and has ensured that both parties know where to seek advice and guidance if they really wish to attempt reconciliation. The court, if it so wishes, can also adjourn proceedings to give both parties further time to decide whether they genuinely wish to make a further effort to prolong their marriage.

At the end of this book can be found names and addresses of various organizations which can help with the process of reconciliation. The best known of these is RELATE.

Alternative Dispute Resolution-conciliation and mediation services

There is a fundamental difference between reconciliation, and those services which offer help, and Alternative Dispute Resolution.

Conciliation is directed towards making parting easier to handle. The role of the conciliator is to sort out at least some of the difficulties between those who have made a definite and firm decision to obtain a divorce.

The process of conciliation can take place either out of court, or in court. In court, conciliation only arises once the process of litigating for divorce has commenced. It is particularly relevant where the future of children is under discussion.

With in-court conciliation, there is usually what is known as a "pre trial review" of the issues and problems which parties to a divorce are unable to settle themselves. Both the court welfare officer and the district judge are involved in this process.

Out of court conciliation and mediation is intended to assist both parties in reaching an agreement at a stage before they arrive in court, or approach the court. The person involved at this stage is usually always professionally trained, a social worker normally, and who will act as go between. Both parties can also use specially trained legal personnel, lawyers, to help them reach an agreement. This process is like the process of arbitration and is intended to make the formal legal proceedings less hostile and acrimonious. The Ministry of Justice provides details about mediation services local to you.

Couples heading to the divorce courts will have to consider mediation before legally separating. As part of reforms included in the Children and Families Act 2014, anyone seeking a court order to resolve a dispute over children, finances or splitting property must attend a "mediation information and assessment meeting".

The Family Mediation Council will help and assist in this area https://www.familymediationcouncil.org.uk. The Family Mediation Council was established in October 2007 and works for greater public awareness of, and access to, family mediation. They work closely with the Legal Aid Agency (LAA) and the Ministry of Justice (MoJ) on family mediation related projects.

Dissolution of a Civil Partnership

A petition can be filed 12 months after the initial registration of a civil partnership but one of four conditions must be proved:

* The other person has behaved unreasonably;
* The parties have been separated for two years and the other party consents in writing;
* The other party has deserted you for a period of two years;
* You have been separated for five years, consent is then not necessary.

Financial Claims

The court has the power to make a financial order for payment of a lump sum, transfer of property, pension sharing order and maintenance.

On the death of a civil partner the rights of succession are the same as those given to the survivor of a marriage.

Marriage (Same Sex Couples) Act 2013

This act makes provision for same sex couples in England and Wales. It makes marriage between same sex couples lawful and equivalent to a marriage between a man and woman. The term husband will include a man married to another man. The term wife will include a woman married to another woman.

Persons of the same sex will not be able to divorce on adultery or have their marriage annulled for non-consummation.

The grounds for divorce between a same sex couple are the same as those between a man and a woman save a divorce cannot be filed on the basis of adultery. There is one ground – that the marriage has broken down irretrievably and then one or more of four facts needs to be proved:

- Unreasonable behaviour of the other person;
- Desertion by the other person for a period of two years or more;
- Two years separation with the other party's consent in writing;
- Five years separation where no consent is needed.

In a same sex marriage, the parties have the same rights to make an application for financial provision. The court has power to make an order for maintenance, lump sum, transfer of property and pension provision.

Commencing Proceedings

Online divorces

it is possible to obtain a divorce online as opposed to using a solicitor. This may be easier if the divorce is uncomplicated but not so possible if the divorce is filled with acrimony and the separation of assets complicated. One site offering online divorce services is www. divorce-online.co.uk. This company offer three levels of divorce action:

Managed divorce service

The online Managed Divorce Service will enable you to have your divorce dealt with quickly and efficiently, as the firm will deal with the whole divorce process for you, meaning you do not need to deal with the courts. This is designed for uncomplicated cases. This is for a fixed fee, currently £189 – 2018.

Managed Divorce with a Financial Consent Order - Fixed Fee

This service involves Divorce-Online handling your entire divorce and the making of a binding financial consent order at court, which will put your financial agreement into legal effect and prevent any future claims.

In order to obtain a consent order, you and your spouse need to have reached an agreement about the division of your finances. You are also advised to obtain one if you have already settled your finances earlier to prevent any possible claims in the future. A pension sharing order is not included as part of this service.

Solicitor divorce with financial consent order

Qualified and experienced family law solicitors will handle your divorce and the making of a financial consent order to put any financial agreement you have reached into legal effect. Any telephone calls, letters and legal advice given by your dedicated solicitor are included in the fixed fee.

All correspondence with the court, your spouse or their solicitor is also included. With all of the above services there is a main requirement that:

- *You need to have been married at least 12 months.*
- *Your ex needs to be likely to agree to the divorce, but we can still deal with your divorce if you are unsure about this.*
- *You must see England or Wales as your permanent home, or be domiciled in England or Wales if you live abroad.*
- You have a valid *ground for divorce*

Using a solicitor

Although this book is primarily about assisting a person to do their own divorce, it is important to examine the role of the solicitor, in the first instance, in order to get an idea of the advantages. You may feel that using a solicitor would be more advantageous than divorcing online.

The amount of advice you will need from a solicitor will depend entirely on the circumstances of your case and the complexities involved. One of the reasons for reading a book such as this is to broaden your knowledge and put yourself in a stronger position to handle proceedings

Most divorces will have two fairly distinct stages - the first step of obtaining the divorce decree (divorce) and the more complicated problems of sorting out property and financial matters and making arrangements concerning children.

As with most county court procedures now, the procedure for commencing divorce and the subsequent steps up to the issuing of a decree is largely paperwork. Provided that the circumstances of your divorce are straightforward then there is no real need to consult a solicitor at all. In the next chapter, I will be discussing the actual procedure and how to obtain a divorce without a solicitor.

It is up to both parties to ascertain the complexity of the divorce before deciding to go it alone. The questions you should be asking yourselves, preferably during a face- to-face meeting, are whether or not the marriage can be ended with the minimum of problems. If you are childless and there is no property at stake and there will be no financial complications then you should be able to proceed without a solicitor.

If, however, you own property and have children and also have life insurance policies and pension schemes etc, then you will need to try to reach agreement concerning the division of these. This is where divorce gets complicated and may entail you requesting legal advice.

The division of your assets is a matter for you but it has to be reached by agreement. I will be discussing financial matters and children later in the book.

One other aspect of do-it-yourself divorce is that it can be time consuming. Some people cannot spare the valuable time involved and will be happier to leave it to a solicitor.

A solicitor will handle the whole matter for you, when instructed, from obtaining initial information to obtaining a decree. Your main input will be to check over the necessary paperwork at each stage, as required and, in certain cases to deliver documents to the court. However, all of this will be done at the request and direction of the solicitor.

Your future arrangements

Whilst not essential to consult a solicitor, it is wise to at least get a view on future arrangements which you have negotiated. This is particularly important when it comes to future tax arrangements.

If it is necessary to ask a court to determine future arrangements, because of the inability of parties to a divorce to agree or negotiate, then a solicitor may need to take charge of the whole process, although not necessarily as the whole court process is designed to assist people to carry out their own divorce without legal help. Remember, the more a solicitor does for you the more it will cost. You should both bear this in mind when beginning discussions.

Your choice of solicitor

Not all solicitors deal with divorce cases, as this is a specialized area. In addition, not all solicitors operate the "Legal Help Scheme" (see below) which provides for legal aid, although post 2013 this has been drastically reduced for divorce cases.

It is always advisable for parties to a divorce to use separate solicitors over divorce. Solicitors, in the main, would prefer to represent one party and not both as this can present certain conflicts of loyalty and interest, particularly where there are antagonisms. The first task is for you to choose a solicitor. This can be done by either consulting business pages or, perhaps better, requesting a list of recommended solicitors from an advice agency, such as the Citizens Advice Bureau.

You may also feel that you will be eligible for legal help and you should ensure that the firm of solicitors that you choose operate this. Solicitors who do operate under legal help will be marked on the list of firms and solicitor's offices often clearly demonstrate their participation in the scheme by a sign showing two people sitting at a table with the words "legal aid" underneath.

When you have decided on a firm of solicitors, you should then contact them to make an initial appointment to discuss the matter. Your decision to allow a firm to act for you is a commercial one, and you will want in the initial stages to determine the costs and timeframe for your divorce. As there are a number of firms you should at first test the market in order to ensure that you are getting the best deal.

How much will it cost?

Although the costs of solicitors can be quite high, you should be able to keep the overall cost to a reasonable level.

With divorce costs and solicitors charges the first thing to know is that there are normally three possible legal issues involved in a divorce:

1) The divorce itself, obtaining the divorce and, more particularly the decree nisi-which enables both parties to remarry if they wish. The cost of divorce in this narrow sense is quite modest as it involves a distinct process, which can also be achieved oneself.

2) Issues involving the matrimonial property-basically deciding who gets what and whether any maintenance will be paid and

so on. The technical phrase for this part of the process is 'ancillary relief'.

3) Issues involving children-access, contact, residence, maintenance etc.

It is the latter two areas that can prove to be quite costly.

If dealing with a straightforward divorce then the costs can, more or less, be fixed. Assuming that the divorce is uncontested, there is a court fee, currently £550 (2018) to issue a divorce petition which has to be paid to the court. There is also a court fee of £45 payable to obtain the decree absolute and, normally, there is an affidavit which needs to be sworn during the proceedings which costs approximately £7.50 in most cases. This means that total disbursements payable to the courts are in the region of £602.50. This cost is not cast in stone as there may be extra cost if, for example, the Respondent (person who received the divorce petition) does not reply and it may be necessary to arrange personal service. After the court fees comes the solicitor's charges, which can be significant. This may vary and you will need to obtain quotes.

Legal Help

As of 1st April 2013, legal aid for divorce cases in England and Wales has been withdrawn by the government and you will no longer be able to obtain legal aid funding for your divorce or family law case unless you are a victim of domestic violence. If you are in Scotland there are different rules.

Check if you can get legal aid

However, you might be able to get some or all of your legal costs paid by the government if:

- you're using it to pay for mediation
- have experienced domestic abuse in the last 5 years
- you're at risk of homelessness - for example, if your ex-partner is trying to throw you out of your home

applying for legal aid

To get legal aid, your legal adviser or family mediator will need a legal aid contract. You can Find a solicitor or mediator with a legal aid contract on GOV.UK. Your legal adviser or family mediator will check if you can get legal aid and apply for you. If you qualify, the legal aid will be paid directly to them.

Going to court quickly if you or your children are in danger

If you need to go to court quickly to keep you or your children safe from your ex-partner, you can ask your solicitor to apply for 'emergency legal representation'. It pays your solicitor and court fees

if you need a fast decision on money, property or children.

If you get emergency legal representation, you should also ask your solicitor to apply for legal aid for any future costs or court hearings.

If you can't get legal aid

You might be able to get other help to pay for legal advice or court representation, including:

- free or low cost advice from a solicitor or caseworker in a law centre
- up to half an hour free from a solicitor
- free advice (known as 'pro bono' advice) from a solicitor, although this is rare for separation cases
- free advice (known as 'pro bono' advice) from a volunteer barrister

Paying less for a solicitor

You might be able to get free or low cost legal advice from a solicitor or legal adviser in a law centre. Find your local law centre on the Law Centres Network. There might not be a law centre near you that covers family issues, but it's worth checking. If you can't use a law centre, see if any solicitors near you offer half an hour of free advice. The Law Society can help you find a local solicitor. Some solicitors offer more than half an hour of free advice, although this is fairly rare for separation cases. Ask your nearest Citizens Advice if they know of local solicitors who offer free advice.   You should research different solicitors before deciding which to choose. Ask them how much they charge and how long they think the process will take. Don't automatically go for the cheapest or the closest. It's important you feel you'll have a good relationship with them.

Paying less for a barrister

If your separation is complicated or needs specialist advice, a solicitor might pass your case onto a barrister. Like a solicitor, a barrister is a type of lawyer so it might be cheaper for you to go straight to a barrister yourself if you think your separation will need specialist advice. You can go directly to a barrister through the public access scheme.

If you need to go to court, you can apply to be represented by a volunteer barrister. You'll need to be referred to one by:

- speaking to your nearest citizens advice bureau
- asking a law centre
- going to a legal advice centre

To get help from a volunteer barrister you need to show you:

- can't afford a barrister - there's no set fee, but they'll normally cost at least £150 an hour
- cant get legal aid

You'll need to apply at least 3 weeks before your next court date.

Help with Mediation

Help with Mediation has its own special rules. It is available only if you are taking part in family mediation or you have successfully reached an agreement with your spouse and need legal advice or support from a solicitor. For example, you may need a solicitor to put your agreement into a legal form so that it can be submitted to the court.

Recovering the cost of divorce from your spouse

It is wise to agree between you beforehand who pays what costs towards the divorce. One of the fundamental principles when handling divorce is to try to sort as much out as possible in order to minimize future complications and also costs, both emotional and financial.

If you cannot decide, or agree, the court will take a view as to who should bear costs. As a general rule, the petitioner will hardly ever be ordered to pay the respondents costs of divorce. A respondent, however, may have to pay a petitioners costs, although not if the petitioner is eligible under the Legal Help Scheme. This depends entirely on the basis for divorce. You can change your solicitor at any point in time if you are unhappy and are paying for the service out of your own pocket. However, you will have to finalize your solicitors bill up to that point. If you feel that you have a complaint then you can complain to the Solicitors Complaints Bureau, set up by the Law Society as part of its regulatory functions. Again, any advice agency will give you details concerning this agency, and how to go about complaining.

The procedure for obtaining a divorce

Whichever way you choose to arrive at your divorce, the underlying procedure is the same. In undefended petitions, both spouses accept that the divorce will go ahead. In defended petitions, one party is filing a defence against the petition.

A special procedure was introduced to deal with undefended divorce petitions, primarily because of the large volume of cases presented to the courts. At present, there is a set pattern, which you must follow if you wish to obtain a divorce:

a) the petition must be filled in (form D8-see appendix)

b) the petition must enclose a statement of arrangements for the children (if appropriate)

c) three copies of the petition(s) must be sent to the registrar of the divorce county court.

d) there must be sufficient copies for the other parties to the divorce (3)

e) the respondent will then receive his or her copies from the court.

f) other parties involved will receive their copies.

g) the respondent must, on a prescribed form (D10) acknowledge service.

h) the respondent must make clear that he or she has no intention to defend.

i) the documents are examined by a court official (the divorce registrar)

j) the divorce registrar then certifies that the facts of the case are approved.

k) the judge pronounces the decree nisi in open court.

l) the decree is made absolute on application by the petitioner.

Each of the above steps will be discussed briefly below.

The preparation of the divorce petition.
Either you, the online company you use or your solicitor will prepare the divorce petition. The forms used to commence a divorce can all be

obtained from the divorce centre local to you. In addition, they can be obtained from the internet (Her Majesty's Courts and Tribunals Service) or from a Citizens Advice Bureau. As discussed in solicitor's costs there is a fee to commence divorce.

The website will provide information concerning fees or this can be obtained from your local divorce centre.

On this form you will record details of your marriage and your children and the grounds on which you are seeking a divorce. You will also list the claims that you are asking the court to consider. This part is particularly important. For example you may wish the court to consider financial matters for you.

Normally, you would include your address on the form but you can make application to the court to leave out your address if this poses any danger to you. It is of the utmost importance that you take care at this stage because you are asking the court to make a very important decision on the basis of information given. You should avoid exaggerating the truth.

A Parenting Plan

It is advisable to put together a Parenting Plan which is a written or online agreement between parents. It helps you record how you will share the care of your child now and in the future. It can easily be changed and is not a legally binding agreement. Making a Parenting Plan is easier if you both agree on why it is a good idea and what you both want for your child. The first part of the Parenting Plan explains your approach to parenting and your general aims.

Using the Parenting Plan

Your plan can be as simple or as detailed as you like. The simpler it is, the easier it is to stick to. It might include day-to-day arrangements, financial arrangements and decisions about the future. It's a good place to store information like medical records and contact details. You probably won't look at it every day, but it is good to have it available to refer to.

The statement of arrangements

If there are children involved you must fill in another document known simply as "statement of arrangements for children" (form D8A). This sets out the arrangements you intend to make for children once the divorce is granted.

A child, for the purposes of the court is any child who is a child of both parties, an adopted child, or any other child who has been treated by both as part of your family. This does not include children boarded out by local authorities or social services or other voluntary organizations.

Although the courts are not generally concerned with the welfare of adult children (over 16) you will be required to give details of children under 18 who are still receiving instruction at an educational establishment or undergoing other training such as for trade or profession.

The information required for the statement of arrangements will be:

a) where the children will live after divorce
b) who else will be residing there

c) who will look after them

d) where they are to be educated

e) what financial arrangements have been proposed for them

f) what arrangements have been made for the other parent to see them

g) whether they have any illness or disability

i) whether they are under the care or supervision of a person or organization (i.e. social services)

When you have completed this form your spouse should be in agreement. If she or he is not then there will be an opportunity at a later stage to make alternative proposals to the court.

Serving the papers on the respondent and the co-respondent

Once the petition has been received by the courts the court office will then send a copy, plus copy of statement of arrangements to the respondent. This is known as "serving" the documents on the respondent. He or she will also receive two other documents from the court-the "acknowledgement of service" (D10) and the "notice of proceedings".

The notice of proceedings informs the respondent that divorce proceedings have been commenced against him or her and that person must acknowledge service within eight days. There are further instructions concerning seeking legal help or filling in acknowledgement personally.

This document, the acknowledgement of service, is self-explanatory and is designed in question and answer form. It is designed to ensure the court that the respondent has received the papers and is fully aware of impending divorce proceedings against them. The court will not proceed with the case until it has received this information.

If you have commenced proceedings on the ground of adultery then the third party, who is known as the co-respondent, is entitled to be notified of the divorce proceedings.

Non-defence of divorce proceedings

Where the respondent does not wish to defend proceedings, the next steps should be quite straightforward. The court will send either you or your solicitor a copy of the completed acknowledgement of service together with copies of two more forms known as "request for directions for trial" (special procedure) and the "affidavit of evidence" (special procedure) The special procedure indicates that the divorce process will be streamlined. Before, all petitioners seeking a divorce had to go to court and give evidence before a judge. This is no longer necessary. Like many county court procedures the route is now simplified and quicker.

The affidavit of evidence, like all affidavits, confirms that what you have said in your petition is true. You will need to "take an oath" in front of a solicitor which is called "swearing" the affidavit. Any questions concerning the truth later could ultimately, if it is discovered that you have lied, lead to contempt of court.

The "request for directions for trial" is a basic form requesting the court to proceed with your case. Both documents, the affidavit and the request for directions are then returned to court.

The case is then examined by an official of the court who will either declare that the facts of the case are proven, or otherwise. If the district judge is happy with the case he or she will issue a certificate that you are entitled to a decree of divorce. Any claims for costs will also be considered at this stage.

When a certificate has been issued, a date will be fixed for decree nisi to be pronounced in open court by judge or district judge. You will be informed of this date but you need not attend court. However, if there is a dispute over costs you will need to attend and the matter will be dealt with by the judge Both the respondent and petitioner are then sent a copy of the decree nisi by the court. However, you have not yet reached the stage of being finally divorced. It is only when your divorce has been made absolute at a later stage that you will be free to remarry if you wish. A decree absolute follows approximately six weeks after decree nisi. If the district judge is not satisfied that you should be granted a divorce, then you will either be asked to produce further evidence or the matter will be sent for trial.

You may be entitled to legal aid if this happens. This is dependent on your income and you should seek advice. If you are refused a divorce, and you have been handling the case yourself then you will most certainly need to go and see a solicitor.

Defence of divorce

If the respondent or co-respondent has returned the papers stating that he or she intends to defend the petition, your next move will be very much dependent on whether an "answer" setting out the defence has been filed. The respondent has 29 days to file a reply.

If a defence has been filed, then the special procedure designed to speed up the process can no longer be used. In this case it is advisable to see a solicitor. There will eventually be a date given for a hearing in court at which both the petitioner and respondent will be expected to attend.

Evidence will be given to the judge who will then have to decide if a divorce should be granted. Legal aid would almost certainly be available and the whole process, depending on the defence can be quite lengthy.

If you are the respondent and you feel that you wish to defend the petition you will almost certainly need to see a solicitor and take advice. In general, undefended straightforward cases, particularly where there are no children involved, can be done on a do-it-yourself basis. Anything more complicated will mean that you will probably need to see a solicitor.

If any other problems arise, such as the respondent either failing or refusing to return acknowledgement of service, proceedings will be delayed whilst a visit by a court official is made. This visit is to ascertain and provide evidence of service. If the respondent cannot be traced, a request can be made to the court for the petition to be heard anyway. Again, this will result in delay.

Ending a civil partnership-procedure

1. File an application

To end a civil partnership, you first need to fill in a dissolution application. (form D8)

You must include your:

- full name and address
- civil partner's full name and address

- civil partnership certificate - the original certificate or a copy from a register office
- Include the names and dates of birth of any children (no matter how old they are).

You must try to find your civil partner's current address if you don't know it. The court will need it to send them a copy of the divorce petition.

Court fee

You will have to pay a £550 court fee to file the dissolution application. You may be able to get help with court fees if you're on benefits or a low income. You can pay by phone with a debit or credit card. The court can call you to take your payment.

Include a letter with your petition to request the call and give them your phone number.

By post with a cheque

Make out the cheque to 'HM Courts and Tribunals Service' and send it with your petition.

Sending the forms

Once you have filled in the forms:

- send 3 copies to the court
- keep copies for yourself
- include your cheque, or your letter asking to pay by phone

Where to send the forms

Send the forms to your nearest court dealing with civil partnership dissolution. The locations of the various courts can be obtained from https://www.gov.uk/end-civil-partnership/file-application

2. Apply for a conditional order

You can get a conditional order if your partner agrees to end the civil partnership. A conditional order is the first of 2 stages to getting the civil partnership dissolved - the second stage is getting a final order.

If your partner doesn't agree to end the civil partnership, you can still apply for a conditional order. You'll have to go to a hearing at the court to discuss the case, where a judge will decide whether to grant you the conditional order.

You must wait at least 9 days after your civil partner has received their copy of the dissolution application.

Fill in the application form

To apply for a conditional order, fill in the application for a conditional order. If your partner is defending the case, fill in section B of the form, saying you want a 'case management hearing' before the judge. You also need to fill in a statement confirming that what you said in your dissolution application is true.

There are 4 statement forms - use the one that covers the grounds you've given for ending the civil partnership:

- unreasonable behaviour statement
- desertion statement
- 2 years' separation statement
- 5 years' separation statement

The forms will need to show your civil partner:

- has received the dissolution application
- agrees to the dissolution if you're using the fact that you've been living apart for 2 years as your reason
- agrees with any arrangement proposed for children

Attach your civil partner's response to the dissolution application, and send it to the court. Keep your own copy.

3. Apply for a final order

The final order is the legal document that ends your civil partnership. You have to wait 6 weeks after the date of the conditional order to apply for a final order. If your civil partner applied for a conditional order, you have to wait 3 months and 6 weeks after the date of the conditional order. Apply within 12 months of getting the conditional order - otherwise you will have to explain the delay to the court. If you want a legally binding arrangement for dividing money and property you must apply to the court for this before you apply for a final order.

To apply for a final order, fill in the application for a conditional order to be made final. A final order costs £45. This fee won't apply if you filed your application after 1 July 2013, as it's now part of the application fee. Return the form to the court with the fee. This will usually be the same court that dealt with your conditional order.

Getting the final order

The court will check that there are no reasons why the civil partnership can't be ended. You must provide all details the court asks for within the time limits. If the court is happy with all the information, it will send you and your civil partner a final order.

Once you get your final order, your civil partnership has ended and you can enter into another civil partnership if you wish. You must keep your final order safe - you will need to show it if you enter into another civil partnership or to prove your status.

If your partner lacks mental capacity
You can apply to end your civil partnership if your partner 'lacks mental capacity' and cannot agree to end the civil partnership or take part in the process. Your partner will need someone to make decisions for them during the process.

The person who acts on their behalf is called a 'litigation friend'. It can be a family member, close friend or someone else who can represent them.

If your partner doesn't have a litigation friend
If there's no one suitable and willing to be their litigation friend, you can apply to the court to appoint a litigation friend. The Official Solicitor may agree to act as your partner's litigation friend when there's no one else to do this ('litigation friend of last resort').

How to apply
Check there's nobody else suitable or willing to act as your civil partner's litigation friend.

Check that there's money available for any costs the Official Solicitor has to pay. Your civil partner may be able to get legal aid.

Give the details of your civil partner's doctor or other medical professional to the court so it can ask for a certificate of capacity.

After you apply

If the Official Solicitor agrees to act as litigation friend for your civil partner, you'll be able to end your civil partnership. To contact the Official Solicitor's staff Email or call the private family law team if you have an enquiry.

ospt.dsm@offsol.gsi.gov.uk

Telephone: 020 3681 2754

****

Chapter 9.

Making a Will and Dealing With Probate

_____

The main principle underlying any will is that, if you have possessions, own property etc then you need to organise a will which will ensure that chosen people benefit after your death.

In the majority of cases, a person's affairs are relatively uncomplicated and should not involve the use of a solicitor.

There are certain basic rules to be followed in the formation of a will and if they are then it should be legally binding.

The only inhibiting factor on the disposal of your assets will be any tax liability following death, which will be dealt with later in this book. There are a number of other factors to consider, however:

• Age of person making a will

A will made by anyone under the age of eighteen, known as a minor, will not be valid unless that person is a member of the services (armed forces) and is on active service.

• Mental health considerations

A will formed by a person, who was insane at the time of writing, will not be valid. Mental illness in itself is not a barrier to creating a will, as long as proof can be shown that the person was not insane at the time of writing. Subsequent mental illness, following the formation of a will, will not be a barrier to a will's validity.

Definition of insanity

Insanity, or this particular condition, will normally apply to anyone certified as such and detained in a mental institution. In addition, the Mental Health Act covers those in " a state of arrested or incomplete development of mind which includes sub-normality of intelligence and is of such a nature or degree that the patient is incapable of living an independent life or guarding against serious exploitation.

In any situation where there is doubt as to a persons capabilities then it is always best to have any will validated by an expert. This applies to anyone, not just those classified as insane.

The main point of any will is that, in the final analysis, a court would have to be satisfied that the contents of the will are genuine, there has not been any attempt whatsoever to alter the contents or to influence that persons mind. The person writing the will must have fashioned its contents with no outside interference.

Unfortunately, the history of the production of people's last will and testament is littered with greedy and unscrupulous persons who wish to gain from another's demise. It is necessary to be careful!

Making a will

The main reason for making a will is to ensure that you make the choice as to who you leave your possessions, and not the state. You can also impose any specific conditions you want in your will. For example, you can impose age conditions or conditions relating to the need to perform certain duties before benefiting.

If you do not make a will then, on your death, the law of intestacy will apply to the disposal of your estate.

The law of intestacy

If a person dies without leaving a will or without leaving a valid will, the laws of intestacy apply. It is important to note that the Inheritance and Trustees Power Act 2014 has introduced changes regarding who will inherit under and intestate estate and also how much they inherit. The changes will have no effect on people who die with assets worth less than £250,000.

The law of intestacy rests on the question of: who survived the deceased?

- If there is a lawful spouse or civil partner and the deceased died leaving children then the spouse receives the first £250,000 in respect of assets solely in the deceased's name plus half of the remaining capital. Children receive half remaining capital, then on the death of the spouse/civil partner the children receive the remaining capital.

- If there is a lawful spouse/civil partner and the deceased died leaving no children, the spouse receives the entire estate. This is a new provision introduced following the introduction of the above mentioned Inheritance and Trustees Powers Act 2014, which came into force in October 2014. the changes apply in England and Wales.

- If there are children, but no spouse or civil partner, everything goes to the children in equal shares.

- If there are parent(s) but no spouse or civil partner or children then everything goes to parents in equal shares.

195

- If there are brothers or sisters, but no spouse or civil partner, or children or parents everything goes to brothers and sisters of the whole blood equally.
- If there are no brothers or sisters of the whole blood, then all goes to brothers and sisters of the half blood equally.
- If there are grandparents, but no spouse or civil partner, or children or parents, or brothers and sisters everything goes to the grandparents equally.
- If there are uncles and aunts, but no spouse or civil partner, or children or parents, or brothers or sisters or grandparents, then everything goes to uncles and aunts of the whole blood equally.
- If there are no uncles and aunts of the whole blood, then all goes to uncles and aunts of the half blood equally.
- If there is no spouse or civil partner and no relatives in any of the categories shown above then everything goes to the Crown.
- A spouse is a person who was legally married to the deceased when he or she died.
- A civil partner is someone who was in a registered civil partnership with the deceased when he or she died. It doesn't include people simply living together as unmarried partners or as common law husband and wife.

The term children includes children born in or out of wedlock and legally adopted children; it also includes adult sons and daughters. It does not, however, include stepchildren.

Brothers and sisters of the whole blood have the same mother and father. Brothers and sisters of the half blood (more commonly referred to as half brothers and sisters) have just one parent in common.

Uncles and aunts of the whole blood are brothers and sisters of the whole blood of the deceased's father or mother.

Uncles and aunts of the half blood are brothers and sisters of the half blood of the deceased's father or mother.

It is important to note that if any of the deceased children die before him, and leave children of their own (that is grandchildren of the deceased) then those grandchildren between them take the share that their mother or father would have taken if he or she had been alive. This also applies to brothers and sisters and uncles and aunts of the deceased who have children – if any of them dies before the deceased, the share that he or she would have had if he or she were still alive, goes to his or her children between them.

The principle applies through successive generations – for example a great grandchild will take a share of the estate if his father and his grandfather (who were respectively the grandson and son of the deceased) both died before the deceased.

It is important to note that if any of the following situations apply to you, or if you are in any doubt whatsoever, you should seek legal advice before distributing the estate of a person who has died without leaving a will:

- The deceased died before 4th of April 1988
- Anyone entitled to a share of the estate is under 18
- Someone died before the deceased and the share he or she would have had goes to his or her children instead
- The spouse/civil partner dies within 28 days of the deceased.

A spouse or civil partner must outlive the deceased by 28 days before they become entitled to any share of the estate.

An ex-wife or civil partner (who was legally divorced from the deceased or whose civil partnership with the deceased was dissolved before the date of death) gets nothing from the estate under the rules of intestacy, but he/she may be able to make a claim under the inheritance (Provision for Family and Dependants) Act 1975, through the courts. Legal advice should be sought if making such a claim.

Anyone who is under 18 (except a spouse or civil partner of the deceased) does not get his or her share of the estate until he or she become 18, or marries under that age. It must be held on trust for him or her until he or she becomes 18 or gets married.

Apart from the spouse or civil partner of the deceased, only blood relatives, and those related by legal adoption, are entitled to share in the estate. Anyone else who is related through marriage and not by blood is not entitled to a share in the estate.

If anyone who is entitled to a share of the estate dies after the deceased but before the estate is distributed, his or her share forms part of his or her own estate and is distributed under the terms of his or her will or intestacy.

Great uncles and great aunts of the deceased (that is brothers and sisters of his or her grandparents) and their children are not entitled to a share in the estate.

Further changes under the Inheritance and Trustees Powers Act 2014

The definition of personal property/chattels has also changed. Under old rules, the term "chattels" was outdated and included old-fashioned terms such as "carriages", "linen" and "scientific instruments". Under new rules "personal chattels" includes all tangible moveable property, apart from property which consists of money or security for money, or property that was used solely or mainly for business purposes or was held solely as an investment

The old definition of chattels will still apply where a Will was executed before 1 October 2014 and makes reference to s55 (1) (x) (Administration of Estates Act 1925).

Under old rules, if an individual died leaving a child under the age of   18, who was subsequently adopted by someone else, there was a risk that the child may lose their inheritance from their natural parent. The new rules ensure that children will not lose any claim to inheritance if they were adopted after the death of a natural parent.

The decision to make a will

It is essential that you make a will as soon as possible. If you leave it, there is a chance that you may never get round to doing it and may be reliant upon the state doing it for you. There is also the chance that you will leave a situation where people start to contest your possessions, fight amongst each other and fall out.

There are many things to consider when you decide to produce a will. As a person gets older, chances are that he or she will become wealthier. Savings grow, endowments increase, insurance policies become more valuable, property is purchased and so on. A bank balance in itself is no indicator of worth, as there are many other elements which add up to wealth. Changes in personal circumstances often justify the need to make a will.

- Ownership of property
- Children
- Marriage or remarriage
- Employment

- Illness
- Divorce and separation
- Increase in personal wealth, such as an inheritance

Ownership of property

Ownership of property usually implies a mortgage. If you are wise it will also imply life insurance to at least the value of the property. It is very prudent to make a will which specifies exactly to whom the property will be left. As we have seen, the law of intestacy provides for the decision if you do not have a will.

Children

As we have seen, under the law of intestacy, any children you have will benefit after your death. However, it is very sensible, under a will, to specify how and when they will benefit. It could be that you may let someone else make that decision later on. Whatever, you should make it very clear in your will.

Marriage or remarriage

The most important point to remember is that marriage or remarriage will automatically revoke the provisions of any former will, although this is not the case in Scotland. Therefore, when marrying you should make certain that your will is up to date and that you have altered the provisions. In short, you should amend your will, or produce a new will in order to outline clearly what you want your new partner to have.

Employment

You should be very aware that certain types of employment carry greater risks than others. This will necessitate producing a will as soon as possible as if you are in a high-risk category then you need to ensure that those nearest you are catered for.

Illness

Illness is something that none of us want but cannot avoid if it decides to strike. No matter how healthy you are you should take this into account when considering putting together a will. In addition, some people have a family history of illness and chances are that they too could suffer. Therefore illness is a very real motivator for producing a will.

Divorce and separation

The law of intestacy states that if you die your divorced spouse loses all rights to your estate. You may not want this to happen and make provisions in your will. Although children of any marriage will benefit it could be that you may wish to make slightly different provisions for different children.

Increase in personal wealth

Financial success, and inheritance will increase your wealth and inevitably make you estate more complicated. It is absolutely essential to ensure that you have a will and that you are updating that will regularly to take into account increased assets.

The provisions of a will

Having considered some of the many reasons for producing a will, it is now necessary to look at exactly what goes into a will. Essentially, the purpose of a will is to ensure that everything you have accumulated in your life is disposed of in accordance with your own desires. The main areas to consider when formulating a will are:

- Money you have saved, in whatever form
- Any buildings (property) you have
- Any land you have
- Any insurance policies you have. This is of utmost importance
- Any shares you may own
- Trusts set up
- Any other personal effects

Money you have saved

Money is treated as part of your wider estate and will automatically go to those named as the main beneficiaries. However, you might wish to make individual bequests to other people outside your family. These have to be specified. When including any provisions in your will relating to money, you should be very clear about the whereabouts of any saving accounts or endowments, premium bonds etc. Life becomes very difficult if you have left sums of money but there is no knowledge of the whereabouts of this. Inevitably, solicitors have to be employed and this becomes very expensive indeed.

Property

It is necessary to make provisions for any property you have. If you are the sole owner of a property then you can dispose of it as you wish. Any organisation with a superior interest would take an interest, particularly if there are mortgages outstanding. It is important to remember that if you are a joint owner of a property, such as a joint tenancy, then on death this joint ownership reverts to the other joint owner, bringing it into sole ownership.

Leasehold property can be different only in so much as the executor of an estate will usually need permission before assigning a lease. This can be obtained from the freeholder.

Land

Although the same principles apply to land as to property, indeed often the two are combined, in certain circumstances land may be owned separately. In this case the land and everything on it can be left in the will.

Insurance policies

The contents of any insurance policy needs to be checked carefully. In certain cases there are restrictions on who can benefit on death. Particular people may be specified and you have no alternative but to let such people benefit, even though your own circumstances may have changed. If there are no restrictions then you can bequeath any money as you see fit.

Shares

Shares can normally be bequeathed in a will as anything else. However, depending on the type of share, it is just possible that there may be restrictions. One such situation is where shares are held in a private company and there may be a buy back clause.

Trusts

Trusts can be set up for the benefit of family and friends. However, a trust, by its very nature is complex as the law dealing with trusts is complex. It is absolutely essential, if you are considering setting up a trust to get specialist advice.

Personal effects

Although you are perfectly entitled to leave specific items of personal effects in your will, such legacies are separate from those of other possessions such as money or land.

The law recognises that in some cases there may not be enough money to pay expenses related to your death. Any money owed will be retrieved from any financial gifts you have outlined. However, personal effects cannot be touched if you have clearly identified these in your will. This includes items of value such as jewellery.

It is not enough to be general on this point. You must specify exactly what it is you are leaving and to whom. Remember, certain gifts will be taxable.

The funeral

It is common practice to include such matters as how you wish to be buried, in what manner and the nature of the ceremony, in your will. You should discuss these arrangements with your next of kin in addition to specifying them in your will as arrangements may be made for a funeral before details of a will are made public. Another way is to detail your wishes in a letter and pass this on to your executor to ensure that the details are known beforehand. There is no reason why any of your instructions should not be carried out, subject to the law. However, your executor can override your wishes if necessary and expedient. You can, in addition, make known your wishes for maintenance of your grave after your death. Agreement of the local authority, or relevant burial authority must be sought and there is no obligation on them to do this. In addition, there is a time limit of 99 years in force.

The use of your body after death

It could be that you have decided to leave your body for medical research or donate your organs. This can be done during your final illness, in writing or in front of a minimum of two witnesses. You should contact your local hospital or General Practitioner about this, they will supply you with more details.

Making a recital

A recital consists of a statement at the end of your will which explains how and why you have drawn up a will in the way you have. This is not commonly done but sometimes may be necessary, especially if you have cut people out of your will but do not intend to cause confusion or hurt.

Recitals are sometimes necessary in order to clarify a transfer of authority to others on your death. This could be in business for example. In addition, you may wish to recognise someone's contribution to your life, for example a long serving employee or a particular friend.

Making provisions in your will

Who to name

When including persons, or organisations, in your will it is better to form a separate list right at the outset.

Naming individuals in your will

There are certain criteria which apply when naming individuals in a will, although in principle you can name who you want. Any person considered an adult, i.e. over 18, can benefit from your will. However, if a person cannot be traced within a time period of seven years after being named, or dies before you, then the amount left in your will to that person is included in what is known as the residue of your estate, what is left after all bequests. You can also make a bequest in your will to cover that eventuality, that is for another named person to benefit in his or her place.

If the bequest is to your own children or any other direct descendant and they die before you then the gift will automatically go to their children, unless there is something to the contrary in your will. In addition, if you make a gift to two or more people and one dies then that share is automatically passed to the other (joint owner).

Children

You are entitled to leave what you want in your will to children whether they are illegitimate or stepchildren. Stepchildren should be stipulated in your will. If children are under 18 then it will be probably necessary to leave property such as land, in trust for them until they reach 18 or any other age stated in the will. No child under 18 can be a trustee. Those people who are not British citizens, i.e. foreigners can benefit from your will in the same way as anyone else.

The only real restriction to this is if there is a state of war between your own country and theirs, in which case it will be necessary to wait until peace is declared.

Mental illness

There is nothing currently in law which prevents a person suffering mental illness from receiving a bequest under a will. Obviously, depending on the state of mind of that person it could be that someone may have to accept the gift and take care of it on the persons behalf.

Bankruptcy

If a person is either bankrupt or facing bankruptcy then if that person receives a gift there is a chance that it could end up in the hands of a creditor. To avoid this happening you can establish a protective trust which will enable the person in receipt of the gift to enjoy any interest arising from the gift during a specific time.

Animals

It is possible to leave money to animals for their care and well-being. There is a time limit involved for receipt of the money, which is currently a period of 21 years.

Groups

There is no problem legally with leaving money and other gifts to groups or organisations. However, it is necessary to ensure that the wording of the will is structured in a certain way. It is necessary to understand some of the legislation concerning charities, in order that your bequest can be deemed charitable.

Leaving money/gifts to charities

Many people leave bequests to charity. Major charities often give advice to individuals and other organisations on how to do that. Smaller charities can pose a problem as they may not be as sound and as well administered as larger ones. It is best to stipulate an alternative charity in the event of the smaller one ceasing to operate. If for whatever reason you bequest cannot be passed on to the group concerned then it will be left in the residue of your estate and could be liable to tax. There are a number of causes which might be deemed as charitable. These are:

- Educational causes
- Help for the community
- Animal welfare
- Help for the elderly
- Disabled
- Religious groups
- Sick, such as hospices

In the event of making a bequest to a charitable cause, it is certain that you will need expert advice, as with the setting up of trusts.

Preparing a will

One of the key rules is that there should be nothing in your will that can be ambiguous or open to interpretation. It is essential to ensure that your intentions are crystal clear. It will probably be necessary to get someone else to look at your will to ensure that it is understood by others.

A will can of course be rewritten. However, it is very important indeed to ensure that you have spent enough time in the initial preparation stages of your will as it could be enacted at any time, in the event of sudden death. If your possessions are numerous then it is highly likely that the preparation stage will be fairly lengthy as the dividing up will take more thought. This gets more complicated depending on your other circumstances, such as whether you are married or single, have children, intend to leave money to organizations, etc.. You need to make a clear list of what it is you have in order to be able to achieve clarity in your will. For example, property and other possessions will take in any buildings and land you own plus money in various accounts or other forms of saving. In addition there could be jewellery and other valuables to take into account. It is necessary to quantify the current value of these possessions. It is also necessary to balance this out by making a list of any outstanding loans/mortgages or other debts you may have. Funeral costs should come into this. It is essential that you do not attempt to give away more than you actually have and also to deduce any tax liabilities from the final amount after debts. The wording of any will is always done with tax liability in mind.

Listing those who will benefit from your will

Making a list of beneficiaries is obviously necessary, including all groups, individuals and others who will benefit. With each beneficiary you should list exactly what it is that you bequeath. If a trust is necessary, then note this and note down the name of proposed trustees. These persons should be in agreement before being named. Contact any charities that will benefit. They can supply you with a legacy clause to include in your will.

The most important point, at this stage, is that you ensure that what you are leaving does not exceed the estate and that, if liable for tax, then there is sufficient left over to meet these liability.

Make a note of any recitals that you wish to include in your will and exactly what you wish to say.

The choice of an executor of your will

The job of any executor is to ensure that your will is administered in accordance with the terms therein as far as is legally possible at that time. It is absolutely essential to ask those people is they consent to being an executor. They may well refuse which could pose problems. You can ask friends or family or alternatively you can ask a solicitor or your bank. They will make a charge for this. However, they are much less likely to make a mistake in the execution of the will than an untrained individual. They will charge and this should be provided for. If you do choose to appoint an untrained executor, then it is good policy to appoint at least two in order to ensure that there is an element of double checking and that there are enough people to fulfill the required duties.

The presentation of your will

You can either prepare your will on ordinary sheets of paper or used specially prepared forms which can be obtained from stationers or book shops. Bookshops will usually sell "will packs" which take you through the whole preparation stage, from contemplation to completion.

Try to avoid handwriting your will. If it cannot be read then it will be invalid. You should always try to produce it on a word processor or typewriter. This can be more easily altered at any time.

The advantage of using a pre-printed form is that it has all of the required phrases on it and you just fill in the blanks. It just may be that you are not in the position to write your will, as you may be one of the considerable numbers of people who cannot read or write in this country. In this case, you can get someone else to write it for you although it is essential that you understand the contents. Get someone else, independent of the person who wrote it to read it back to you to ensure that the contents reflect your wishes.

Safekeeping of a will

A will must always be kept safe and should be able to be located at the time of your death. You may spend a great deal of time on your will. However, if it cannot be found then it will be assumed that you have not made one.

Wills and the courts

Courts have wide powers to make alterations to a persons will, after that persons death. It can exercise these powers if the will fails to achieve the intentions of the person who wrote it, as a result of a clerical error or a failure to understand the instructions of the person producing the will. In addition, if mental illness can be demonstrated at the time of producing the will then this can also lead to the courts intervening.

In order to get the courts to exercise their powers, an application must be made within six months of the date on which probate is taken out. If gifts or other are distributed and a court order is made to rectify the will then all must be returned to be distributed in accordance with the court order.

If any part of a persons will appears to have no meaning or is ambiguous then the court will look at any surrounding evidence and the testators intention and will rectify the will in the light of this evidence.

Former spouse

There is one main condition under which a former spouse can claim and that is that they have not remarried. In addition, such a claim would be for only essential maintenance which would stop on remarriage. There is one key exception, that is that if your death occurs within a year of divorce or legal separation, your former spouse can make a claim.

Child of the deceased

As the above, any claim by children can only be on the basis of hardship.

Stepchildren

This includes anyone treated as your own child and supported by you, including illegitimate children or those conceived before, but not born till after, your death. The claim can only cover essential maintenance.

Dependants

This covers a wide range of potential claimants. Maintenance only is payable. There needs to be evidence of full or partial maintenance prior to death. Such support does not have to be financial, however.

There is another situation where the court can change a will after your death. This relates directly to conditions that you may have imposed on a beneficiary in order to receive a gift which are unreasonable. If the court decides that this is the case, that particular condition becomes void and does not have to be fulfilled.

If the condition involved something being done before the beneficiary receives the gift then the beneficiary does not receive the gift. If the condition involved something being done after the beneficiary received the gift then the beneficiary can have the gift without condition.

If the beneficiary does not receive the gift, as in the above, then either the will can make alternative provision or the gift can form part of the residue of the estate. Unreasonable conditions can be many, one such being any condition that provides reason or incentive to break up a marriage, intention to remain celibate or not to remarry or one that separates children. There are others which impinge on religion, general behaviour and crime. An unreasonable condition very much depends on the perception of the beneficiary and the perception of the courts. A beneficiary can lose the right to a bequest, apart from any failure to meet conditions attached to a bequest. Again, a court will decide in what circumstance this is appropriate. Crime could be a reason, such as murder, or evidence of coercion or harassment of another person in pursuit of selfish gain.

Probate

Probate simply means that the executor's powers to administer the estate of a dead person have been officially confirmed. A document called a "Grant of Representation" is given which enables those administering the estate to gain access to all relevant information, financial or otherwise concerning the person's estate.

Although anyone charged under a will to act on behalf of the dead persons estate has automatic authority to represent, there are certain cases where evidence of probate is required. If no will exists or no executors have been appointed, then it will be necessary to obtain "letters of administration" which involves a similar procedure.

Under common law, probate has a number of objectives. These are:

- To safeguard creditors of the deceased
- To ensure reasonable provision is made for the deceased's dependants
- To distribute the balance of the estate in accordance with the intentions of the person whose will it is.

One of the key factors affecting the need to obtain probate is how much money is involved under the terms of a will. Where the sums involved are relatively small then financial institutions and other organisations will not normally want to see evidence of probate. However, it should be remembered that no on is obliged to release anything relating to a dead persons estate unless letters of administration or documents of probate can be shown. Those responsible for administering the estate must find out from the organisations concerned what the necessary procedure is.

Applying for probate

Where a will is in existence and executors have been appointed then any one of the named people can make the application. Where a will is in existence but no executors have been appointed, then the person who benefits from the whole estate should make the application. This would be the case where any known executor cannot or will not apply for probate. Where there is no will in existence then the next of kin can apply for probate. There is an order of priority relating to the application:

- The surviving spouse
- A child of the deceased
- A parent of the deceased

- A brother or sister of the deceased
- Another relative of the deceased

The person applying for probate must be over eighteen. 'Children' includes any that are illegitimate. If a child dies before the deceased then one of his or her children can apply for probate.

Application for probate

This can be done through any probate registry or office. There is usually one in every main town and any office in any area will accept the application. If you are writing then you should always address your correspondence to a registry and not an office. You can also contact the Probate Registry and Inheritance Tax Helpline 0845 302 0900 or visit the website www.justice.gov.uk which deals with matters of probate.

What needs to be done next

The next of kin should register the death with the register of Births and Deaths. A death certificate will be supplied and copies of the death certificate which will need to be included to various institutions and organisations.

A copy of the will has to be obtained. The whereabouts should be known to the executors. The executor should then take a copy of the will in case the original is lost. The executor will need to obtain full details of the dead persons estate, including all property and other items together with a current valuation. It is possible that on many of the less substantial items a personal valuation can be made. It should however, be as accurate as possible.

In the case of any bank accounts a letter should be sent by the executor to the bank manager, stating that he is the executor and giving full details of the death. Details should be requested concerning the amount of money in the dead persons account(s) together with any other details of valuables lodged with the bank. The bank manager may be able to pass on information concerning holdings in stocks and shares. If share certificates are held then a valuation of the shares at time of death should be requested.

In the case of insurance policies, the same procedure should be followed. A letter should be sent to the insurance company requesting details of policies and amounts owed or payable.

In the case of National Savings Certificates the executor should write to the Savings Certificate Office in Durham and ask for a list of all certificates held, date of issue and current value. In the case of Premium Bonds a letter should be sent to the Bond and Stock Office in Lancashire Giving name and date of death. Premium Bonds remain in the draw for 12 months after death, so they can be left invested for that time or cashed in when probate has been obtained. Form SB4 (obtained from any post office) is used to inform of death and obtain repayment of most government bonds.

In the case of property, whatever valuation is put on a property the Inland revenue can always insist on its own valuation. If there is a mortgage, the executor should write to the mortgagee asking for the amount outstanding at the time of death.

The above procedure should be followed when writing to any one or an organisation, such as a pension fund, requesting details of monies owed to the dead person.

216

Debts owed by the person

The executor will need to compile a list of debts owed by the dead person as these will need to be paid out of the estate. These debts will include all money owed, loans, overdrafts, bills and other liabilities. If there is any doubt about the extent of the debts then the executor can advertise in the London Gazette and any newspaper which circulates in the area where the estate is situated. Efforts also have to be made to locate creditors outside of advertising. The advert will tell creditors that they have to claim by a certain date after which the estate will be administered having obtained probate.

Funeral expenses should be quantified and a letter should be sent to HM Revenue and Customs to determine the income tax position of the dead person.

Finally

The executor obtains the application form, decides where he or she wishes to be interviewed, send the completed form together with the death certificate and the original will to the Probate Registry and then attends for an interview.

****

Chapter 10

Landlord and Tenant-The Law Generally

Explaining the law

It is very important for both landlords and tenants to understand the rights and obligations of respective parties to a tenancy and exactly what can and what cannot be done once the tenancy agreement has been signed and the property is occupied.

Some landlords think they can do exactly as they please, because the property belongs to them. Some tenants do not know any differently and therefore the landlord can, and often does, get away with breaking the law. However, this is not the case, there is a very strong legal framework governing the relationship between landlord and tenant and it is important that both parties have a grasp on the key principles of the law.

In order to fully understand the law we should begin by looking at the main types of relationship between people and their homes.

The freehold and the lease

In law, there are two main types of ownership and occupation of property.

These are:

* freehold and;
* leasehold. These arrangements are very old indeed.

Freehold

If a person owns their property outright (usually with a mortgage) then they are a freeholder. The only claims to ownership over and above their own might be those of the building society or the bank, which lent them the money to buy the place. They will re-possess the property if the mortgage payments are not kept up with. In addition, the Crown can exercise rights in times of war, for example.

In certain situations though, the local authority (council) for an area can affect a person's right to do what they please with their home even if they are a freeholder. This will occur when planning powers are exercised, for example, in order to prevent the carrying out of alterations without consent.

The local authority for your area has many powers and we will be referring to these regularly.

Leasehold

If a person lives in a property owned by someone else and has a written agreement allowing them to occupy the flat or house for a period of time i.e., giving them permission to live in that property, then they will, in the main, have a lease and either be a leaseholder or a tenant of a landlord.

The main principle of a lease is that a person has been given permission by someone else to live in his or her property for a period of time. The person giving permission could be either the freeholder or another leaseholder.

The tenancy agreement is one type of lease. If you have signed a tenancy agreement then you will have been given permission by a person to live in their property for a period of time.

The position of the tenant

The tenant will usually have an agreement for a shorter period of time than the typical leaseholder. Whereas the leaseholder will, for example, have an agreement for ninety-nine years, the tenant will have an agreement, which either runs from week to week or month to month (periodic tenancy) or is for a fixed term, for example, six-months or one-year. These arrangements are the most common types of agreement between the private landlord and tenant. The agreement itself will state whether it is a fixed-term or periodic tenancy. If an agreement has not been issued it will be assumed to be a fixed term tenancy. Both periodic and fixed-term tenants will usually pay a sum of rent regularly to a landlord in return for permission to live in the property (more about rent and service charges later)

The tenancy agreement

The tenancy agreement is the usual arrangement under which one person will live in a property owned by another. Before a tenant moves into a property he/she will have to sign a tenancy agreement drawn up by a landlord or landlord's agent. *A tenancy agreement is a contract between landlord and tenant.* It is important to realize that when you sign a tenancy agreement, you have signed a contract with another person, which governs the way in which you will live in their property.

The contract

Typically, any tenancy agreement will show the name and address of the landlord and will state the names of the tenant(s). The type of tenancy agreement that is signed should be clearly indicated. This could be, for example, a Rent Act protected tenancy, an assured tenancy or an assured shorthold tenancy. In the main, in the private sector, the agreement will be an assured shorthold.

Date of commencement of tenancy and rent payable

The date the tenancy began and the duration (fixed term or periodic) plus the amount of rent payable should be clearly shown, along with who is responsible for any other charges, such as water rates, council tax etc, and a description of the property you are living in.

The landlord must also serve a notice stating the address to where any legal notices can be sent. In addition to the rent that must be paid there should be a clear indication of when a rent increase can be expected. This information is sometimes shown in other conditions of tenancy, which should be given to the tenant when they move into their home. The conditions of tenancy will set out landlords and tenants rights and obligations.

Services provided under the tenancy and service of notice

If services are provided, i.e., if a service charge is payable, this should be indicated in the agreement. The tenancy agreement, as stated, should indicate clearly the address to which notices on the landlord can be served by the tenant, for example, because of repair problems or notice of leaving the property. The landlord has a legal requirement to indicate this.

Tenants obligations

The tenancy agreement will either be a basic document with the above information or will be more comprehensive. Either way, there will be a section beginning "the tenant agrees." Here the tenant will agree to move into the property, pay rent, use the property as an only home, not cause a nuisance to others, take responsibility for certain internal repairs, not sublet the property, i.e., create another tenancy, and various other things depending on the property.

Landlords obligations

There should also be another section "the landlord agrees". Here, the landlord is contracting with the tenant to allow quiet enjoyment of the property. The landlord's repairing responsibilities are also usually outlined.

Ending a tenancy through a ground for possession

Finally, there should be a section entitled "ending the tenancy" which will outline the ways in which landlord and tenant can end the agreement. If it is an assured shorthold tenancy then a Form 6A notice will be served to end the tenancy naturally, the same for ending on a ground, such as rent arrears (Form 6A has replaced s21 and s8 notices for all tenancies from October 1st 2018) more about this later). It is in this section that the landlord should make reference to the "grounds for possession". Grounds for possession are circumstances where the landlord will apply to court for possession of his/her property. Some of these grounds relate to what is in the tenancy, i.e., the responsibility to pay rent and to not cause a nuisance. Other grounds do not relate to the contents of the tenancy directly, but more to the law governing that particular tenancy. The grounds for possession are very important, as they are used in any court case brought against the tenant. Unfortunately, they are not always indicated in the tenancy agreement. As they are so important they are summarized later on in this chapter.

It must be said at this point that many residential tenancies are very light on landlord's responsibilities. Repairing responsibilities, and responsibilities relating to rental payment, are landlord's obligations under law. This book deals with these, and other areas. However, many landlords will seek to use only the most basic document in order to conceal legal obligations.

The public sector tenancy (local authority or housing association), for example, is usually very clear and very comprehensive about the rights and obligations of landlord and tenant. Unfortunately, the private landlord often does not employ the same energy when it comes to educating and informing the tenant.

Overcrowding /too many people living in the property

It is important to understand, when signing a tenancy agreement, that it is not permitted to allow the premises to become overcrowded, i.e., to allow more people than was originally intended, (which is outlined in the agreement) to live in the property. If a tenant does, then the landlord can take action to evict.

By the same token, landlords are faced with new regulations (since 2017 – see below) that they do not create overcrowding. Rogue landlords will be banned from cramming tenants into tiny box rooms in a government initiative to improve housing standards. Rooms must be no smaller than 70sq ft for a single person and 110sq ft for couples, under new rules announced by the Department for Communities. Rogue landlords who rent out substandard properties face being forced out of the sector as new banning orders are brought in and a national database of offenders went live on 6th April 2018.

The crackdown comes after an investigation by a newspaper last year found rogue landlords converting two or three bedroom terraced homes into bedsits that house eight or more strangers, each paying £400 to £500 a month for a room. Animal infestations are common and many of the homes have unsafe electrics and are damp. Fire precautions are mostly non-existent. Such overcrowding has caused tensions within communities with neigbours complaining of noise and anti-social behaviour and rubbish over-flowing from small front yards.

Councils will be able to use revenue from the licence fee to enforce the higher standards, with fines of up to £30,000 for the worst offenders.

Different types of tenancy agreement
The protected tenancy - the meaning of the term

As a basic guide, if a person is a private tenant and signed their current agreement with a landlord before 15th January 1989 then they will, in most cases, be a protected tenant with all the rights relating to protection of tenure, which are considerable. Protection is provided under the 1977 Rent Act. In practice, there are not many protected tenancies left and the tenant will usually be signing an assured shorthold tenancy.

The assured shorthold tenancy - what it means

If the tenant entered into an agreement with a landlord after 15th January 1989 then they will, in most cases, be an assured tenant. We will discuss assured tenancies in more depth in the next chapter In brief, there are various types of assured tenancy. The assured shorthold is usually a fixed term version of the assured tenancy and enables the landlord to recover their property after six months and to vary the rent after this time. At this point it is important to understand that the main difference between the two types of tenancy, protected and assured, is that the tenant has less rights as a tenant under the assured tenancy. For example, they will not be entitled, as is a protected tenant, to a fair rent set by a Rent Officer.

Other types of agreement

In addition to the above tenancy agreements, there are other types of agreement sometimes used in privately rented property. One of these is the company let, as we discussed in the last chapter, and another is the license agreement. The person signing such an agreement is called a licensee.

Licenses will only apply in special circumstances where the licensee cannot be given sole occupation of his home and therefore can only stay for a short period with minimum rights. There is one other type of agreement that is not widely used and that is the Common law tenancy.

Common Law Tenancies

These are tenancies that fall outside the scope of the Housing Acts (1988, 1996, 2004), which includes the Regulated Tenancies, Assured Tenancies (AT) and Assured Shorthold Tenancies ASTs.

In the case of common law tenancies, the tenant's rights and obligations are mainly dependent on the terms agreed between the parties (written into the agreement), and therefore similar to a commercial lease; they are contractual or "non-statutory contractual tenancies" as opposed to those being regulated by statute.

Commercial (business tenancies) are similar, but businesses have the added protection of the Landlord and Tenant Act 1954, which affords some security of tenure (succession rights) for a businesses on renewal – when the fixed term comes to an end.

Any residential tenancy where the rent equates to an **annual rate in excess of £100,000 pa** (previously £25,000 set in 1990 and increased in October 2010) is excluded from the Housing Act Tenancy (AT or AST) rules and therefore must be a common law tenancy.

Alternatively, where a limited company rents a residential property (usually for their employees) the tenancy will fall outside the scope of the Housing Acts – again it's a common law tenancy.

225

Often, companies rent residential accommodation and let the property to their employees, usually under a licence agreement (as opposed to a tenancy). Often the employee pays rent and other costs to the landlord, but ultimately the company is liable.

Joint Tenancies and The Common Law Tenancy

A rental rate of £100,000 pa may seem quite a lot, but this also applies to join tenancies where the combined rent of all the sharers (such as students) is included in this total - £8333.33 per month is the limit.

Implications for Landlords – Common Law Tenancies

The implications of common law tenancies are:

(1) a different tenancy agreement from the usual AST will be required, and

(2) any deposit taken is not subject to the requirements of the Deposit Protection Scheme under the Housing Act 2004.

(3) the rules governing re-possession under the Housing Acts do not apply.

Security of Tenure – Common Law Tenancies

Common Law Tenancies do not afford tenants the same protection regarding security of tenure and statutory continuation as do Assured Tenancies (including Shorthold Assured Tenancies).

Therefore the AST section 21 and section 8 notices and possession procedures do not apply, and the letting operates on the literal wording of the Tenancy Agreement. Similarly, the Deposit Protection (DPS Scheme) rules do not apply. However, the Protection from Eviction Act 1977 still applies, meaning that in the case of a common law residential tenant refusing to leave, a court order will be required.

Bringing a Common Law Tenancy to an End

With a Common Law tenancy the landlord is entitled to possession at the end of the fixed-term. In theory the landlord is not required to serve a notice to quit to bring the tenancy to an end as the tenancy ends at the agreed date, but in practice the landlord should serve a notice if he wishes the tenant to vacate.

Also, if there are problems during the tenancy, the landlord can bring the common law tenancy to an end where there has been a breach of any of the specified terms in the tenancy agreement. He is not restricted to the prescribed terms (grounds) laid down in Housing Acts.

Statutory Protection for Common Law Tenants

A residential common law tenant still has some statutory protection in that they cannot be evicted against their will unless the landlord obtains a court order (Protection from Eviction Act 1977).

Common Law Tenants will also get protection under the Unfair Terms in Consumer Contracts Regulations 1999, where they have entered into a standard form (pre-printed) tenancy agreement.

They will also benefit from some other statutory provisions including the landlord's repairing obligations under the Landlord and Tenant Act 1985.

Squatting

Under section 144 of the Legal Aid, Sentencing and Punishment of Offenders Act, which came into force on the first day of September 2012, squatting in residential buildings (like a house or flat) is illegal. It can lead to 6 months in prison, a £5,000 fine, or both. Squatting is when someone knowingly enters a residential building as a trespasser and lives there, or intends to live there.

A tenant who enters a property with the permission of the landlord, but who falls behind with rent payments, is **not** a squatter. Although squatting a non-residential building or land isn't in itself a crime, trespassers on non-residential property may be committing other crimes.

It's normally a crime for a person to enter private property without permission and refuse to leave when the owner asks. In certain circumstances, it may also be a crime if someone doesn't leave land when they've been directed to do so by the police or council, or if they don't comply with a repossession order.

Squatting in non-residential properties

A non-residential property is any building or land that isn't designed to be lived in.

Simply being on another person's non-residential property without their permission is not usually a crime. But if squatters commit other crimes when entering or staying in a property, the police can take action against them. These crimes could include:

- causing damage when entering the property
- causing damage while in the property
- not leaving when they're told to by a court
- stealing from the property
- using utilities like electricity or gas without permission
- fly-tipping
- not complying with a noise abatement notice

Getting a non-residential property back

If a person owns the property that has been squatted, he or she can use an interim possession order (IPO) to get their property back quickly.

If the right procedure is followed, they can usually get one issued by the courts within a few days. To get final possession of the property, they must also make an application for possession when they apply for the IPO.

Use form N130 to apply for an interim possession order and for possession.

Exceptions

You can't use an IPO if:

- you're also making a claim for damages caused by the squatters - instead you can make an ordinary claim for possession
- more than 28 days have passed since you found out about the squatters
- you're trying to evict former tenants, sub-tenants or licensees Once squatters are served with an IPO, they must leave the property within 24 hours. If they don't, they're committing a crime and could serve up to 6 months in prison.

It's also a crime for them to return to the property within 12 months.

Squatters taking ownership of a property

It's difficult and very rare for squatters to take ownership of a property. To do this, they would have to stay in a property without the owner's permission for at least 10 years.

****

Chapter 11

Taking Back Possession of a Property

Fast-track possession

A landlord cannot serve a s21 notice (Form 6A) on an assured shorthold tenant until after the first four months of a tenancy (if it is for a six month period). This brings the tenancy to an end on the day of expiry, i.e. on the day of expiry of the six month period,

Rules for Section 21 notices

If the tenancy started or was renewed on or after 1 October 2015 a landlord will need to use the new prescribed Section 21 notice Form (6a). Form 6A has replaced both S21 and S8 Notices although the Form still relates to S21 and S6 of the Housing Act.

Section 21 (Form 6A) pre-requisites

A landlord cannot serve a valid Form 6A notice if:

- They have taken a deposit and not protected and/or served the prescribed information and/or
- They have failed to obtained a license for an HMO property which requires one

If the tenancy was in England and started or was renewed on or after 1 October 2015 a landlord must also have served on their tenant (and you should get proof of service for all these:

- an EPC
- a Gas Safety Certificate, and
- the latest version of the Government's "How to Rent" Guide.
- Which deposit scheme the tenants deposit is in

Plus a landlord cannot serve a section 21 notice if their Local Authority has served one of 3 specified notices (the most important being an improvement notice) on them within the past six months in respect of the poor condition of the rental property.

Also, if the tenant complained about the issues covered by the notice prior to this – any Section 21 notice served since the complaint and before the Local Authority notice was served will also be invalid.

The notice period must not be less than two months and must not end before the end of the fixed term (if this has not ended at the time the landlord served their notice)

If this is a periodic tenancy where the period (rent payment period) is more than monthly (e.g., a quarterly or six month periodic tenancy), then the notice period must be at least one full tenancy period.

The notice period does not have to end on a particular day in the month, as was required under the old rules – the landlord just needs to make sure that the notice period is sufficient – minimum of 2 months.

On expiry of the notice, if it is the landlord's intention to take possession of the property then the tenants should leave. It is worthwhile writing a letter to the tenants one month before expiry reminding them that they should leave.

In the event of the tenant refusing to leave, then the landlord has to then follow a process termed 'fast track possession'. This entails filling in the appropriate forms (N5B) which can be downloaded from Her Majesty's Court Service Website www.justice.gov.uk.

Assuming that a valid Form 6A notice has been served on the tenant, the accelerated possession proceedings can begin and the forms completed and lodged with the court dealing with the area where the property is situated. In order to grant the accelerated possession order the court will require the following:

- The assured shorthold agreement
- The section 21 notice (Form 6A)
- Evidence of service of the notice

The best form of service of the Form 6A notice is by hand. If you have already served the notice then evidence that the tenant has received it will be required. Having the correct original paperwork is of the utmost importance. Without this, the application will fail and delays will be incurred.

If the tenant disputes the possession proceedings in any way they will have 14 days to reply to the court. If the case is well founded and the paperwork is in order then there should be no case for defence. Once the accelerated possession order has been granted then this will need to be served on the tenant, giving them 14 days to vacate. In certain circumstances, if the tenant pleads hardship the court can grant extra time to leave, six weeks as opposed to two weeks. If they still do not vacate then an application will need to be made to court for a bailiffs warrant to evict the tenants.

Accelerated possession proceedings cannot be used against the tenant for rent arrears. It will be necessary to follow the procedure below.

An accelerated possession order remains in force for six years from the date it was granted.

Going to court to end the tenancy

There may come a time when a landlord needs to go to court to regain possession of their property. This will usually arise when the contract has been breached by the tenant, for non-payment of rent or for some other breach such as nuisance or harassment. As we have seen, a tenancy can be brought to an end in a court on one of the grounds for possession. However, as the tenancy will usually be an assured shorthold then it is necessary to consider for the landlord to consider whether they are in a position to give two months notice and withhold the deposit, as opposed to going to court. The act of withholding the deposit will entail the landlord refusing to authorize the payment to the tenant online. This then brings arbitration into the frame. Deposit schemes have an arbitration system as an integral part of the scheme.

If a landlord decides, for whatever reason, to go to court, then any move to regain a property for breach of agreement will commence in the county court in the area in which the property is. The first steps in ending the tenancy will necessitate the serving of a notice of seeking possession Form 6A using one of the Grounds for Possession detailed earlier in the book. If the tenancy is protected then 28 days must be given, the notice must be in prescribed form and served on the tenant personally (preferably).

If the tenancy is an assured shorthold, which is more often the case now, then 14 days notice of seeking possession can be used. In all cases the ground to be relied upon must be clearly outlined in the notice. If the case is more complex, then this will entail a particulars of claim being prepared, usually by a solicitor, as opposed to a standard possession form.

A fee is paid when sending the particulars to court, which should be checked with the local county court. The standard form which the landlord uses for routine rent arrears cases is called the N119 and the accompanying summons is called the N5. Both of these forms can be obtained from the court or from www.courtservice.gov. When completed, the forms should be sent in duplicate to the county court and a copy retained for you.

•The court will send a copy of the particulars of claim and the summons to the tenant. They will send the landlord a form which gives them a case number and court date to appear, known as the return date. On the return date, the landlord should arrive at court at least 15 minutes early. Complainants can represent themselves in simple cases but are advised to use a solicitor for more contentious cases.

If the tenant is present then they will have a chance to defend themselves.

A number of orders are available. However, if you a person has gone to court on the mandatory ground eight then if the fact is proved then they will get possession immediately. If not, then the judge can grant an order, suspended whilst the tenant finds time to pay.

In a lot of cases, it is more expedient for a landlord to serve notice-requiring possession, if the tenancy has reached the end of the period, and then wait two months before the property is regained. This saves the cost and time of going to court particularly if the ground is one of nuisance or other, which will involve solicitors.

In many cases, if landlords are contemplating going to court and have never been before and do not know the procedure then it is best to use a solicitor to guide the case through.

Costs can be recovered from the tenant, although this will depend on their means. If possession is regained midway through the contractual term then the landlord will have to complete the possession process by use of bailiff, pay a fee and fill in another form, Warrant for Possession of Land.

If a landlord has reached the end of the contractual term and wish to recover their property then a fast track procedure is available which entails gaining an order for possession and bailiff's order by post. This can be used in cases with the exception of rent arrears.

****

Ch.12

The Law and Neighbours

The majority of people live peaceably with their neighbours. In fact, good relations with neighbours is essential for the maintenance of a healthy and balanced community. However, it is also the case that, at times, relations with neighbours break down and people turn to the law to obtain justice.

It is an unfortunate fact, particularly in the large urban centres, such as London, that people can live for years in a street and not know their neighbours. People become landlords and let their properties, which can lead to disruption if the incoming tenants are anti-social and do not have strong ties to an area.

The law strikes a balance when dealing with neighbour disputes. On one hand, people are free to use their property as they wish. On the other, it is essential that the rights of others are respected when we decide to embark on a course of action in our own property.

There are specialist organisations, based on mediation, who try to resolve disputes without recourse to the law. These organisations are usually within local authority areas, are free and can resolve disputes through mediating with the parties involved. See useful addresses for addresses of mediators.

In law, we both have a 'duty of care' and a duty to be reasonable to our neighbours. Essentially, this duty is to treat a person or people with the same degree of care and respect that we would expect to be afforded. It is when this is not the case that the law comes into play.

Neighbours and noise complaints

Of all the complaints that neighbours level against each other, the most common is that of noise. Noise can arise from many different sources, crying babies, footsteps and general movement, parties, dogs and so on. In each case, the law would recognise a reasonable level, over which legal action is seen to be reasonable. Generally, the local environmental health department of the council would provide measurements of noise and would determine what is reasonable. One main problem that has arisen is that of inadequate sound proofing, particularly in converted flats and new build properties. Builders have tended to construct properties with a minimum level of soundproofing that has proved to be inadequate.

In all disputes with neighbours, resorting to the law should be the last course of action. There are a number of other alternatives to consider first. It is always best to try to solve problems amicably. In the long run this proves the most fruitful as you will likely be neighbours for a long time to come and you will want to maintain good relationships.

The first thing to do is to talk to your neighbours and to establish what the nature of the problem is and whether your neighbours can acknowledge that there is a problem and do something about it. It might also help to speak to other neighbours and see whether they are also affected in the same way.

It is advisable to keep written records of the noise, a diary of sorts, recording the nature and type of noise and the frequency. This is the only way to create a tangible body of evidence.

Contacting landlords

If you feel that you cannot solve the problem by approaching the people concerned then it may be necessary to contact a landlord. The nature of a landlord can have a bearing on a person's ability to solve a case, whether the landlord is a social landlord, i.e. a housing association or local authority or private landlord. In many cases, the person creating the noise will also be an owner-occupier.

Social landlords

If the landlord of a person or people creating a noise is a social landlord, i.e. a housing association or local authority, the first thing that you should do, having tried to solve the problem amicably and started to keep a diary, is to contact the landlord and lodge a complaint, making it clear that you are maintaining a diary. The landlord will have signed a tenancy with the person involved and part of that tenancy agreement will be a covenant that the tenant does not cause a nuisance or annoyance to his/her neighbours. The landlord will contact the tenant and will begin the process whereby, ultimately; the tenant could be evicted for breach of tenancy.

However, it is important to realise that taking such action successfully can be a long and difficult process and it may be easier to take your own action, or at least take your own action in conjunction with the landlord.

Environmental Health Departments

The 1990 Environmental Protection Act (EPA) is the guiding framework within which environmental health officers operate. An individual can go direct to the Environmental Health Department, as can a landlord. In addition, the Environmental Health Department can also take action against individuals without waiting for a complaint to come in. To compliment environmental health, a landlord, particularly social landlords, can use independent witnesses to back up other bodies. Some local authorities operate 'noise patrols' which are intended to back up other evidence.

The EHO (Environmental Health Officer) will usually write a letter to the offending person, which will serve as a warning. If this does not work, then the EHO will write a letter stating that the individual is in breach of Section 80 of the EPA and, if the noise is not abated then the matter can become a criminal offence with a fine and/or prison sentence attached to it.

Using the Magistrates Court

There are other alternatives to the Environmental Health Department. A person suffering noise nuisance can go to the Magistrates court, under section 82 of the Environmental Protection Act 1990. Before you do so you have to give your neighbour formal written warning of your intention to take the matter to the magistrate's court, and this may well be sufficient to stop the noise. If it does not, then you have to fill in the appropriate forms, which can be obtained from the magistrates court, and make an appointment for a hearing. The court will need to be satisfied that a genuine noise nuisance exists and that you have made an effort to solve it directly with your neighbour.

If they are satisfied then they will issue a 'noise abatement order' and it becomes a criminal offence to breach this order.

Using the county court

Going to the county court is another alternative. You could begin a civil action in a county court to obtain an injunction to stop noise. The complaint must, however, be serious and the noise intolerable to obtain an injunction. Injunctions are expensive and difficult to obtain and the burden of proof that much greater. If you are attempting to obtain an injunction then you will almost certainly need a solicitor.

Owner-occupiers and noise

If you own your own property and the person causing the nuisance is also an owner-occupier them you will not have a landlord to complain to, unless the person is a leaseholder. If the person is a leaseholder then you should establish who the freeholder is, i.e. who built and sold the property and insist that this person takes action under the lease. In addition to this, you should complain to the Environmental health officer of the Local Authority or go to the magistrate's court in order to attempt to stop the noise.

If the person is a freeholder, and there is no landlord then you can only pursue the remedies described, i.e. EHO or magistrates court.

You could try contacting the police. However, unless the problem is domestic violence or some other criminal offence, the police are reluctant to get involved.

Other sources of noise

There are many sources of noise, in particular street noise, that cannot be pinpointed to a neighbour but nevertheless cause distress to others.

One such source of noise is that of car alarms. In addition, builders and others operating in the streets can also cause noise nuisance.

In order to combat the problems of street noise, a Noise and Statutory Nuisance Act came into effect in 1994 and extends the scope of the Environmental Protection Act 1990, so that street noise is also classified as a statutory nuisance. The Act covers nuisance from vehicles, machinery or equipment in the street. It deals in particular with car alarms and burglar alarms. The concept of 'street' covers not only roads but also pathways, square or court open to the public. It does not mater whether the area is private or public. 'Equipment' includes musical equipment and even ice cream vans and buskers.

The exclusions

The Act does not apply to traffic noise, political demonstrations or noise made by any 'naval, military or air force'.

Car alarms

The person responsible for a car with a faulty alarm is the person who is the registered owner of the vehicle, or any other person who, for the time being, is responsible for the vehicle. An Environmental Health Officer can serve an abatement notice on that person to remedy the fault. The EHO can serve a notice on the vehicle and, if after an hour nothing further has been done or the person responsible has not been found, the EHO can either immobilise the alarm or remove the vehicle. The EHO has powers to open and enter a car, causing as little damage as possible. It must also be secured against theft when the EHO has completed the task.

House alarms

Householders have to inform local authorities of alarms that they intend to install. The alarm must meet prescribed requirements and the police must be informed of any key holders and of their telephone numbers. If any alarm is still operating one hour after it has been set off, then an officer of the local authority can enter and turn off that alarm providing that he or she has permission to do so. If no permission from the owner is forthcoming then a warrant can be obtained from a justice of the peace to enter the premises, if necessary by force, as long as damage is kept to a minimum and the premises is secured. The owner can be called upon to reimburse the authority for any cost incurred.

Problems with boundaries and fences

There is no absolute rule of law that requires a person to mark a boundary of his or her property or to enclose it with a fence. However, even if there are no rules, it is always advisable to reach agreement with neighbours about boundaries. If you are buying a property, always try to ensure that the boundaries are clearly marked and that it is clear what land you will own. Ascertain rights of way and car parking, if appropriate. Be very wary of buying a property where the plan does not tally with what you actually see on the ground. If in doubt contact the boundary skills panel of the Royal Institution of Chartered Surveyors (see useful addresses).

Plans

In general, with any conveyance of land there should be a plan. annexed to the title deeds, which is supposed to show where the boundaries to a property lie. However, a plan can be inaccurate,
242

misleading or out of date. If you have not established the boundaries before you move in and trouble arises from a neighbour, the question is, what is the remedy?

The objective test

In general, the court will take an objective view, i.e. what are the facts? The court will look at the plan but will also look at all the surrounding circumstances that have resulted in the situation arising. On many occasions, there will be a trip arranged to the disputed are in order to ascertain the nature of the problem.

Fences

Even where there is no demarcation dispute between neighbours a frequent source of tension can be responsibility for the upkeep of fences.

Who owns the fence and who should keep it in repair?

General rules regarding ownership

There are certain assumptions about responsibility for fences. Generally, where title deeds do have a plan then that plan will demark any fence ownership and if the 'T' mark used to demark the fence falls on your side then you will be responsible. If there is no 'T'mark or no plan then there is a general assumption that you own the fence if the supporting posts are on your land.

Party fences

You can decide to have a party fence with both sides owning the fence and both sides contributing to the costs of repair. This is usually prevalent where ownership cannot be ascertained. Part wall legislation will generally find that both parties are responsible for the upkeep.

Mending fences

In general, if a fence belongs to a neighbour he or she is not under a legal duty to repair it. You can only insist on repair if it represents a hazard to your land and property. In this case, you can approach an environmental health officer and lodge a complaint under the Environmental Health Act. If you need to repair the fence at your own expense because it is a danger, you will need your neighbour's permission to go on to his/her land, otherwise you are trespassing. Otherwise, you would have to go to court for leave to go onto the land.

Party walls

In theory, a neighbour on each side of a party wall owns half the wall, whether the division is made vertically or horizontally. Where two buildings have been standing for 20 years or more, each neighbour acquires a right, called an easement, against the neighbour on the other side for the right of support to their property.

General duty to take care

It is reasonable for the law to impose a duty to take care on the owner of a party wall, so that whether he uses it, removes it, builds on it, or repairs it he must minimise the possibility of damage to neighbouring property. In addition, allowing a party wall to fall into disrepair can cause a nuisance and an adjoining owner can sue for damages.

Problems with nuisance generally

There are three types of nuisances, or categories of nuisance in law:

- private nuisance
- public nuisance
- statutory nuisance

Private nuisance

A private nuisance has been defined as something that occurs on someone else's property, which detrimentally affects your property or your enjoyment of your own property. Equally, something that happens on your property can be a source of nuisance to your neighbour. As we have discussed, the first course of action to be taken when dealing with private nuisance is that of approaching your neighbour and trying to find a remedy. Only then should there be recourse to the law.

The Environmental Protection Act 1990 is the Act that regulates nuisance. However, with private nuisance, Environmental Health officers are reluctant to get involved unless the nuisance is prolonged and severe.

Public nuisance

A public nuisance is something that detrimentally affects a large group of people and not only an individual. It often concerns obstructions on the highways.

Statutory nuisance

Certain types of nuisance are covered by legislation. In particular, the Environmental protection Act 1990 has laid down various matters associated with property. As the name of the Act suggests, the law is primarily concerned with those who use their property in such a way as to cause a potential health hazard. The Act refers to the state of the premises, smoke, fumes, dust and any accumulation or deposit of substances that could be prejudicial to health or could cause a nuisance.

It is the well being of the population as a whole that the Act is concerned with. However, you can use its provisions for the protection of your own well being by notifying your local authority of apparent breaches. The local authority has to take steps to remedy a breach, by investigating a complaint and warning a perpetrator if there is cause to do so. If the matter has to be taken further then the Act provides for a series of steps that ultimately lead to criminal action and a fine or imprisonment if found guilty.

Problems with gardens

Overhanging plants and trees

The general rule is that you are entitled to your own space, in and above (to some extent) your own property. So branches from neighbours trees or shrubs which overhang your garden are intrusions into your space, therefore they can be regarded as trespass and nuisance. You are entitled to lop off branches which intrude over your side of the fence. You are supposed to return the branches to your neighbour (and any growth such as fruit). However, in these cases, it is better to negotiate with your neighbour before taking action. If you need to gain access to someone else's property to deal with tress and shrubs then you have the right to apply to court under the Access to Neighbouring Land Act 1992 to allow you to solve the problem.

Obviously, this is extreme and is usually done where the landlord cannot be found or identified.

The same rules apply to roots that are growing into your property and are causing damage. You can cap those roots, as long as the tree is not damaged or you can apply to court for an injunction to prevent any further growth and also sue for damages.

****

Chapter 13.

The Police-Getting Arrested and Making a Complaint Against the Police

_____

There are many reasons why the police might arrest a citizen, a few of those are:

- Driving offences
- Burglary
- Carrying offensive weapons
- Fighting
- Drink and drugs

If the police suspect that you are carrying offensive weapons or other illegal items or substances, they can stop and search without a warrant. If this happens then you can ask to see identification and you have the right to ask why you are being stopped and searched. The police do not have the right to intimidate or bully you.

Search of premises or home

The police have powers to search a premises or a home if they feel that evidence against you found there can help them with their enquiries. They can search a premise's with the consent of an occupier, or a warrant can be obtained from a magistrate to further their enquiries. They can search any premises without a warrant on a number of occasions such as:

- To capture an escaped prisoner
- To protect life or to stop serious damage to property
- Arrest someone for an arrestable offence or public disorder offence
- After an arrest to search a detained persons premises

Many other laws give police powers to enter premises, i.e. terrorism, harbouring an escaped convict and so on. Someone is allowed to be present when the search is taking place unless they might hinder the investigation. The police should give information about their powers to search premises. They are not allowed to use unreasonable force and a record must be kept of the search..

You have no legal obligation or duty to help the police with their enquiries. The only way the police can force you to accompany them to the police station is to arrest you. The police can arrest a suspect by obtaining an arrest warrant from a magistrate. The magistrate will need to be convinced that there is a case against a suspect.

Police also have powers of arrest without a warrant in the following circumstances:

- An arrestable offence (one carrying a potential five-year sentence) has or could have been committed
- Certain other specific offences have been committed such as rape, car theft, shoplifting or other theft offences

- If you are drunk or fail a breath test
- If you are soliciting or living off immoral earnings
- If you refuse to give details of your name and address if a particular law requires you to do so
- Where a breach of the peace has occurred or may occur.

What to do if you are arrested

It may be possible to avoid being arrested if you co-operate with the police in the first instance. However, if you are arrested, then you should be informed of your right to see a solicitor. It does not matter what time you are arrested, the duty solicitor scheme will mean that a solicitor will be on call and will speak to you over the telephone or come out to see you.

You should also be told that you have the right to inform some other person of your arrest. You should be told that you have a right to see the codes of practice followed by the police. You should be given a written note of the three rights above, which will contain the usual caution:

'You do not have to say anything, but it may harm your defence if you do not mention when questioned something which you later rely on in court. Anything you do say may be given in evidence'.

This caution means that you have the right of silence. You do not have to say anything, in particular until a solicitor arrives. In very limited cases, the right of silence has been removed. What you say can be used in any legal proceedings that are brought against you.

It is generally wise to say nothing until a solicitor arrives and then the interview can be guided professionally. What you do say is tape-recorded.

Detaining suspects

If you have not been arrested then the police cannot keep you at the police station. When you have been arrested you should be charged with an offence within 24 hours (usually) or released. You can be held up to 36 hours for a serious offence. If the police wish to detain you for longer than this then they can apply to a magistrate's court for permission to do so. 96 hours is usually the maximum amount of time. The Police and Criminal Evidence Act (PACE) deals with rights when arrested.

Assuming that you have been charged with an offence then you will already have seen a solicitor. If you have not seen a solicitor then it is very wise to do so as they can guide you through the procedure and ensure that what takes place is fair.

After you have been charged, you will either be remanded in custody or let out on bail. If you are remanded in custody you will not be released until after the trial. Bail applications are not, or should not, be refused unnecessarily. However, you may have to provide sureties and comply with certain conditions such as reporting to the police station.

More minor offences are tried in the magistrate's court and more serious offences in the Crown Court. (See previous chapters).

You will need to prepare your case with your solicitor for the trial. There may be witnesses to locate and also statements to prepare. At the trial, you will either be found guilty or not guilty. If you are found not guilty there may be grounds for you to bring proceedings against the police for false imprisonment arising from your original arrest. If you are found guilty then you will be sentenced and at this stage any previous convictions are brought to light.

Once you have been convicted, you will have a criminal record. Some offences are so minor and commonplace that they are unlikely to affect your future employment or well being generally. However, more serious offences can have a serious effect and you should certainly take professional advice. Criminal records arising from different types of crime will last for different periods of time.

Making a complaint against the police

If you think you have been treated unfairly by the police or the standard of service you received was unacceptable you have the right to make a complaint.

Who can make a complaint?

- the victim.
- persons adversely affected.
- witnesses.

If you are making a complaint on behalf a person listed above, you will need to have their written permission. However, this does not apply if you are the parent or guardian of a child aged 16 or under and wish to complain on their behalf, or are a solicitor or MP complaining on someone's behalf.

Who can I complain about?

- police officers.
- special constables.
- all police staff, including PCSOs, PEO staff, detention officers, traffic wardens, administrative staff.

What can I complain about?

You can make a complaint if you:

- experienced inappropriate behaviour from a police officer, staff member, contractor or volunteer. For instance, if you felt they were rude or aggressive in their treatment of you.
- saw a police officer, staff member, contractor or volunteer acting inappropriately.
- have been adversely affected by the conduct of a police officer, staff member, contractor or volunteer, even if it did not take place in relation to you.

You can also complain about how a police force is run. For example, you can complain about policing standards or policing policy.

Who do I complain to?

If you want to make a complaint about the way that your case has been handled by the police, or about any policy or procedure then you should contact your local force. Please note that any complaints sent to the Independent Office for Police Conduct (IOPC) are forwarded automatically to the local police force. The IOPC, which oversees the police complaints system in England and Wales, only investigates the most serious and sensitive incidents and allegations involving the police, for example:

- allegations of serious corruption or serious assault.
- where there are indications of police officers or staff committing criminal offences or causing serious injury.
- where a person's direct or indirect contact with the police may have caused or contributed to their death or injury.

How long do I have to make a complaint?

There is no time limit for making a complaint, although you should try to do it as quickly as possible. This is because when complaints are made a long time after the incident, it can be more difficult to obtain evidence and accurate witness statements. A police force can decide not to deal with a complaint if they receive it more than 12 months after the incident. If you are complaining more than 12 months after an incident, you should explain why your complaint has been delayed. Your police force will need to consider your explanation when they decide whether to deal with the complaint.

How do I make a complaint?

Each force will have its own procedures in place for making complaints; details will be provided on their website. Most police forces will offer the following methods of making a complaint:

- via their online complaints form;
- via the 101 non-emergency telephone number;
- by post to their Professional Standards Department;
- in person at your local police station;
- via the IOPC's online contact form (your complaint will be automatically forwarded to the local force); or
- via a solicitor or MP who can make a complaint on your behalf.

What if I am not happy with the result of my complaint?

When you are informed of the outcome of your complaint, you may be able to appeal. Appeals will be normally be dealt with by the local force, but the IOPC may become involved depending on the seriousness of the matter.

Useful Addresses and Websites
The Legal system
Free Representation Unit
London Office
5th Floor Kingsbourne House
229-231 High Holborn
London WC1V 7DA
www.fru.org.uk
020 7611 9555

Nottingham Office
Nottingham Law School Legal Advice Clinic
Chaucer Building
Chaucer Street
Nottingham NG1 5LP
01158 484 262

The Law Society
020 7242 1222
ww.lawsociety.org.uk

Legal Action Group
National Pro Bono Centre
Royalty Studios
105-109 Lancaster Road
London
W11 1QF
020 7833 2931
http://www.lag.org.uk/

National Association of Citizens Advice bureau
http://www.citizensadvice.org.uk/

Solicitors Regulation Authority
The Cube
199 Wharfeside Street
Birmingham
B1 1RN
0370 606 2555
www.sra.org.uk

Law and the Consumer

Advertising Standards Authority
http://www.asa.org.uk

Association of British Travel Agents
30 Park Street
London SE1 9EQ
www.abta.com

Consumers Association
2 Marylebone Road
London NW1 4DF
020 770 7000
which. co. uk

Consumer Credit Association (UK)
85B Bowen Court
St Asaph Business Park
St Asaph
LL17 OJE
www.ccauk.org

Direct Selling Association
Unit 14-Mobbs Miller House-Christchurch Road
NN1 5LL
01604 625700
http://www.dsa.org.uk/

Children and the Law

Childline
NSPCC
Weston House
42 Curtain Road
London EC2A 3NH
www.childline.org
0800 800 5000 (adults)
0800 1111 (children and young people)

Child Support Solutions
152 Grove Lane
Timperley
Altrincham

Cheshire
WA15 6PD
03456 588683
www.childsupportsolutions.co.uk

The Children's Society
Whitecross Studios
50 Banner Street
London EC1Y 8ST
0300 303 7000
email: supportercare@childrenssociety.org.uk
www.childrenssociety.org.uk

Divorce

Relate
www.relate.org.uk
0330 100 1234
www.relate.org.uk

****

Index

259

****